FORMS OF LIFE

and other essays

REVISED

J.D. Gill

CreateSpace
2014

For my Teachers

Contents

Forward 9

Experience 11

Climbing Through 27

Gender. 57

Little Myths and Stories . . 95

Mr. Cho 121

The Two Sectors and
The Problem of Power . . 193

The Mormons 229

The Old and the New . . . 333

Forms of Life 371

About the Author . . . 461

Forward

This collection of essays is based on a sensibility informed by linguistic analysis and post-modern logic. Recent developments in gender studies as well as psychoanalysis are included. Both the overwhelming importance of an increased focus on language in relation to objects as well as the de-centering effect of monolithic views of knowledge have produced a "new world view." These essays reflect some effects of looking through such a lens.

Special thanks to Michelle Taggart Reedy, M.S.

EXPERIENCE

Rahmana liba bai
[God wants the heart]

--Talmud

There is an experience in walking down a street that is not captured in a description of what one sees. There is the *being there*. Actually being in it. This is why it is so inadequate to prepare for a foreign visit by reading about it.

11

Yet when we are there, where are we? What do we see? How much? Which things? Against which backgrounds are we able to interpret things? Experiences?

I went to Firenze with a friend, who had led me to believe he was well traveled. As we were walking in front of the Duomo in that city, he said: "Well, this certainly isn't Walmart."

Huh?

Where in the hell did that come from? I wondered. You thought Italy would be like Walmart? Is Walmart your base of comparisons for the world? How did you even *have* such a thought, let alone decide to speak it? Is that a yuck-yuck, you-know-we're-Americans sort of comment? Am I supposed to laugh? Such thoughts bombarded me.

But what *was* his experience? What did he see?

As our time together went on I learned he had not really been abroad before--in the sense of substantially getting into a culture and its ways. This was, in effect, a first trip for him. He had only

12

rolled across the surface previously, enclosed in the bubble of his own base.

Of course the trick for all of us is to find a way beyond where we are now. But we have no experience of that which is beyond where we are now. We are thus in the position of seeing and making sense out of the new in terms that really only apply to the old. This is how we can, if you will, be on the street without really being on it.

Like learning a new language, it is a magical experience when one first has a dream in the new language. Something has shifted.

One studies a new book. It is an author one has not read. One reads the book and has a reaction. What reaction does one have? Why? One studies secondary sources, and one's views begin to deepen. One reads the book a time or two more, making new discoveries each time. One talks to other readers. What was their experience? One reads more work from this author. One, as they say, begins to get *into it*.

What does it mean that Joyce sometimes wrote in dramatic style as opposed to narrative?

And, beneath--or behind, all this are our assumptions. They form our *grounding* viewpoints.

As such they are part of many grounding viewpoints, scarcely an eternal truth (for everyone). Nor are we the center of very much at all.

This means that to understand another we have to learn their assumptions. That is we have to find some way to grasp their base and their experience. Their, if you will, Walmart.

In this enterprise it is easy to see that the more adept we are at functioning beyond our own base, the more capable we will be in developing resonance with others.

Some people were raised in homes where others really tried to connect with them and also sought to share themselves with each other. Some people were raised in homes where no one tried to resonate with them or honestly disclose genuine thoughts and feelings.

These people will have different senses of "ordinary." An interaction comfortable for one may drive another crazy.

Further, intimacy depends on developing an open mutual emotional resonance. It is, as Rilke said, "[When] two solitudes protect and meet and greet each other [zwei Einsamkeiten einander schützen, grenzen und grüßen] (see Rilke)."

The failure to establish resonant intimacy results, as Benjamin (1988) pointed out, in domination--which is a move of power rather than understanding.

In thinking about awareness we might imagine vertical and horizontal planes. Vertically, one starts with the ABC's and progresses to a graduate major. One amasses a greater amount of knowledge as well as an increased breadth of knowledge. One begins to learn where one is *not*.

Horizontally, one studies different fields, one is in relationships and families, and one is outside them. One travels the world and experiences wide cultural differences. One's awareness of different contexts expands.

Thus there is development that improves on one's base, and there is development that seeks to shift bases.

The experience of seeing one's base from a different perspective can be profound. One way this happens is by allowing ourselves to be honest and open with someone who does *not* react the way our parents did. For example what was "very bad" at home is now "nothing." This difference in experience allows for the realization things could be different. One's assigned position in one's past is not necessarily one's assigned position in the universe.

Back to the street. If the street I am walking is not my original street, I can be sure it is someone's original street. And, as such, it feels more "right" to them than it does to me. My original street might seem weird to them, &c.

Perhaps I have experience on streets of a hundred of the world's cities to compare with the experience of this particular street. Perhaps it is a street I have always dreamed to visit. Perhaps it is a street of some major tragedy.

How do I couch it? Do I respond to its beauty or charm? Do I think about the laborers who built it? Do I think of the history it has witnessed? Do I wish I could show it to someone I once knew? Does it mean little to me in the context of the city that contains it? Is it the main reason I came to this city? Perhaps I take a photo. Perhaps I think about the transience of life.

I bring a friend: "I want to show you this amazing street." In response she says, "Its okay." Or she says, "What does it mean to you?" Or she says, "You truly are a case." Or she says, "Well, it doesn't look like Walmart."

I develop a fancy for the *Prelude and Fugue in E Flat Major*. I listen to several recordings and note the differences in the performances. I go to a recital to hear it live. The organ is fantastic, newly completed and shipped from Germany. The performance is actually quite good. And there is something here, in this church, with the sound in the live air that is different from my recordings, no matter how good they are. There is something *present* here. I can even feel it.

How would I tell someone about this? What base would he or she use to interpret what I was saying? Would I describe it? Try to evoke it? Hum a few bars?

Curiosity itself is such an amazing thing. Some people are loaded with it. Some have very little. What is this about?

Is one content to stay where one is, or is one *dying* to find out what's *over there*?

One who usually reads fiction decides to dive into Bavarian history or statistics. One takes up the guitar, is determined to master Moroccan cooking.

All one's peers are behaviorists. One pursues psychoanalysis.

And what about the pressure of the peer group? One's high school training to fit at any cost? When one "buys" acceptance in a club by getting it right, what is the cost in terms of one's own truth?

When one works for a corporation and goes to staff meetings, what is the price of agreement?

When one fits in one's neighborhood, what is one doing? Why?

The camaraderie we experience on the team exists at what level of depth or honesty? What do we give up or forego to be there? What if the team were to hold a meeting together and require members to bring their parents along? Their children? What would be different then?

I get closer with one of my peers. He invites me for dinner. I learn more. I invite him. We become friends. We share a space. A street. We meet there. Our lives are richer.

I befriend the clerk at Starbucks. We trade lies and distortions. We lighten each other's day.

I climb the hill silently on my bike and stay to watch the early sunset. It is pale tonight. A young man rides up. "Nice bike," I say.

Is this how we become a collage, a representation of ourselves in a social context? Is this as close as we are allowed to get? Why is this?

Why can't we get closer? Is it because we need to belong, or we need to compete?

We are molded to fit our contexts, and then we struggle to leave them. If we stay--to be a good team player, say--we blind ourselves. If we live so we are understandable to the team, we hobble ourselves.

If, on the other hand, one transcends every context, one finds him or herself in an isolation. And while this allows one to avoid regional narrowness, it can be crippling from the standpoint of interpersonal "correction."

We are essentially social creatures, and, as the object-relations people tell us (see Gabbard, 2000, Ogden, 1990, Bollas, 1987), we are always in relationship with someone--either in or out of our minds.

In the absence of ongoing meaningful human exchange, it is easy to get caught up in one's own views and distortions--and misperceive others as well as oneself.

Of course one cannot know where one is unless one also knows where one is not. Further, and increasingly in our world, both forms of experience must not be cursory fly-overs but genuine attempts to see contexts and people as much as possible *from their own base*. And it is equally important to try to see one's own base from another base.

Stephan Zweig (see Prochnik) said one can no longer simply be a citizen of a country. One must become a citizen of the world. He was in Brazil at the time. Seeing.

And what of tenderness? What of that opening and coming to matter of another and with another? What country is that?

We let each other in. It is an experience profoundly beyond ourselves, and it transforms us. It is such an amazing place. It is so far beyond staff meetings or bike rides. It is strong, and yet it seems so fragile in the world we have.

Without such an experience, who are we?

21

Perhaps we are each persons with some degree of breadth, of expansion. Love expands us, college expands us, travel expands us, parenthood expands us, disaster expands us, tragedy. Rapture expands us, dark nights of misery. Books.

We are always inside or outside of something. We are eager to move, or we are eager to defend our space and stay where we are. Perhaps we compete, so the competition will fill up our time and we will forget about what lies beyond it.

We enter a store. There are people with many different "expansion histories." Is it likely we will be able to get very close? I think not. We decide to find the friendly ones. We smile. We are pushed out of the way by those too busy for the likes of us. Some are welcoming. Some are threatened. Some couldn't care less.

Such experiences are interpreted in terms of the particular viewpoint we have. Who do we consider ourselves to be? (What is our "self-representation?") Who do we consider them to be? How do we know these things? Upon what experiences are they based?

So in the afternoon, in the middle of life, one has an experience of that life. It is the experience one's preparation allows one to have. One is in a library, say, surrounded by its silence, its rows and rows of books. Lenten spring is trying to begin. Something immense is open in the silence and its call is certain.

And there is, as well, the call from what lies beyond such an experience, such richness. This other is beyond grasping in this place. Like unheard overtones, however, it is present in the room and colors the sound that can be heard. There is always that space beyond the present. And as well, the significance of each.

It reminds me of Shakespeare.

> Thou art thy mother's glass, and she in thee
> Calls back the lovely April of her prime.

REFERENCES

Benjamin, J. The Bonds of Love: Psychoanalysis, Feminism, and the Problem of Domination. Pantheon. 1988.

Bollas, C. The Shadow of the Object: Psychoanalysis of the Unthought Known. Columbia. 1987.

Gabbard, G.O. Psychodynamic Psychiatry in Clinical Practice. Third Edition. APA, 2000.

Ogden, T. H. The Matrix of the Mind: Object Relations and the Psychoanalytic Dialogue. Aronson. 1990.

Prochnik, G. http://quarterlyconversation.com/stefan-zweigs-world-of-yesterday

Rilke, R.M. http://www.scribd.com/doc/7817737/Rainer-Maria-Rilke-Letters-to-a-Young-Poet

Shakespeare, W. Sonnet Number Three, in Harri-
son, G.B. (Ed.) Shakespeare: Major Plays and the
sonnets. Harcourt. 1948.

CLIMBING THROUGH

> No problem can be solved from
> the same level of consciousness
> that created it.
>
> --Albert Einstein

There is an old saying: "the grass is always greener on the other side of the fence." That is: life always looks better somewhere else. Actually, life may not be as good as it looks across the fence, but one thing is for certain: it will be different.

This is a way of saying the context is different across the fence than it is here. Thus, the *experience* of being across the fence will be different from the experience of being here.

The world in which we live is made up of an enormous number of different contexts. Each of these function as a base of experience for those who live within them. Thus, people have different experiences of the world depending upon which context they inhabit.

In order to experience another context, I have to leave my own context and go to another one. This, however, is not as easy as it sounds.

Not having first hand experience of another context from my own, I may assume all people there are essentially the same as those in my context. What else should I assume? I can only know what I know. And I use what I know in making judgments about the world. But what I know about my own context is not designed to be accurate in dealing with another context. Therefore I will make errors of judgment and I will miss nuances that likely matter

Obviously, I can try to forget everything I can about my own context and try as best I can to involve myself in the new context. I might, for example, move from New York to Rome with the intent to change cultures. I may do everything I can to shed the old and adopt the new. This enterprise will be more or less successful, depending upon my perceptual skills and flexibility, but, clearly, some part of the old will remain within the new. There is no other way.

The German poet Rilke said No matter how hard you try to wipe off the make-up, some little piece remains behind to betray you (Rilke, 1949).

Another option is to make no effort whatsoever to embrace the new context in its own right. I may continue to steadfastly see it through a lens designed for my original context. For example, I might be in Paris and mock it as being weird, as I can't find an American bar.

I might even take up experiencing contexts as a project--trying as best I can to treat them all equal.

That is, I might try to place myself within each one and experience as many as I can, noting their differences and similarities. I might strive for the goal of "holding" them all in my mind--or whatever portion of this goal I might be able to achieve.

Let's go back to the original context.

One's original context is made up of one's physiology, one's parents, and the surround. When we are born, these three factors immediately come into play.

Clearly, there are innumerable ways in which physiologies differ. Some are complete; some not. Some work well; some not. Some are healthy; some not. There are different skin colors, gender, intellectual capacities, athletic or physical capacities, and different temperaments.

There are also a myriad of different ways in which parents differ--roughly as many ways as there are parents themselves. What are my parents like? What were their parents like? How do they think about me--how do they "hold me in their minds?"

How do they treat me? How do they try to connect with me, if they do? How central am I to their daily focus? And what are their dreams for me? What is their language, and what are their professions? What is their education, and what are their passions? What is my attachment pattern?

The surround is both micro and macro. There is my house, my room. This is where I begin to experience "the world." What are these things like? Is there enough money? Is there play? Is there athletic equipment? Are there books and music? Are there friends who visit? Family? Is it a big city? Is it rural? Do I have siblings? What are they like? How do they see and treat me? What is my sub-culture? Is it open? Closed?

All of these things go into making up the "world" I experience. It will be my first (and perhaps the only) world I know. My developing brain will wire to it. It is this world I will try to master as I develop into a self. It will form my "bedrock." And it will always be firmly there, at least in my unconscious.

As I grow from this beginning, my experiences will become a blizzard of complexity. They will be reduced to some agreed upon themes. People will develop a sense of who I am, as I will myself. These views will be more or less accurate. Slowly I will develop a sense of self, an identity, based in a large part on these experiences.

My position in the family, my position in school, my position with friends and classmates, and my position in the society will all make a profound impact on me.

And, once I have these things down, I will be able to function as an adult in the society and, hopefully, to succeed.

I might go away to college. This will be a major shift as it will require moving to a different context, one I do not know, one with which I have no experience. I won't even have an (internal) map. Such a move will be easier or more difficult, in part, due to how my original context has prepared me for *difference*. Have I experienced different contexts before? Have my parents encouraged me to see my original context as one in a large field of different contexts? Or is their experience, and teaching, limited to the original context?

Going off to college is not the only contextual difference I will experience.

It is a different context to be a Kindergarten student than it is to be a high schooler. It is a different context to be pre-pubescent than it is to be mature. It is a different experience to work for a living than not to, &c.

Thus there is a large array of differences even within "one" context.

Not to mention the fact that an inside view and an outside view are never the same. That is, the view of a context from within and the view of that same context from without will differ in several important ways.

This is like saying the view within a family and without it are not the same. The view within a sub-culture and without it are not the same. The view within a country and without it are not the same, &c.

Additionally, time is a factor. Time is always moving and thus changing the context. This year is not the same as last year--or ten years ago. Ten years from now will be different. Everything is in flux, and therefore everything is constantly seen from different contextual positions.

Quickly, the context issue becomes exotically complex.

Yet one of the best ways to gain an understanding of each of us is through our contexts.

This is where the outside view/inside view difference comes into play.

A therapist, being another person, will necessarily be outside my context. He or she will have come from a different life than mine. Assuming he or she has developed analytic and empathic skills, he or she will be able to see me both from the outside and (to varying degrees) from the inside as well.

Of course there is the issue of being "accurate" and the issue of being "accurate enough." It may be said "accurate enough" is "enough" for a therapist to be a "good enough" therapist.

The procedure of seeing such a therapist will be impactful, because the therapist will be able to notice elements in my account of my context I may not have noticed--that I may never have noticed. They simply have been too familiar. He or she may also be surprised by the role I was assigned by my parents or my school. This will help me see that such a role is not an "eternal truth," but simply something idiosyncratic to my particular context.

There is an old saying that "the fish will be the last thing to discover the water."

Why is this the case? Water is simply all around. The fish is so submerged in the water that there is no contrast in terms of which it may discover the water. There is, if you will, no not-water. Noting something requires contrast. It is the same with us as people. We don't notice the character of our contexts, as we have nothing with which to meaningfully contrast them. Lacking this contrast, we are unable to understand where we are.

Unless we know where we are not, we cannot know where we are. I am in New York City; I am not in Brussels. Having been to Brussels, I have some sense of the world beyond New York City. I very well remember it is different there.

Some experiences are life changing. One is the experience of love. Experiencing love opens the world in ways that cannot be experienced any other way. Having someone else's life mean that much to you, changes everything. As does the experience of being a parent. People who are parents are very different as a rule than are people who have not been parents.

Going to college changes one's perspective in ways not possible to achieve in other ways. As does traveling in other countries. The view of one's culture from outside is sobering. And the experience of how countries and cultures differ from each other--and yet are all forms of the human experience--reshapes the sensibility.

Akin to traveling to different countries is the endeavor to study different fields.

The point here is that the experience of multiple contexts is dramatically different from the adherence to one context alone. There is a sensibility that comes from multiple experiences that leads to a welcome stance in the face of diversity. It is a stance that is not only broadening to one's experience, but it is rapidly becoming essential for survival.

Primitive persons gathered together in groups in order to survive (Eliad, 1963, Campbell, 1986, 1999). One's group was able to defend itself against other groups and devise a method of survival. With the development of city-states, the need to survive shifted to the larger group. City-States organized cultures and means of protection against one another. Here, the strength of the body polititic was critical to survival.

We now live in a different sort of context. We have developed a world that is rapidly requiring city-states to work together instead of in opposition--for the survival of all. This requires a means of cooperation instead of protective fragmentation. In short, rather than a mythology of each, we need to develop a mythology for the whole.

In such a situation the ability to understand and be empathic with differences is critical. No longer is it desirable to wall oneself off and function as one entity against the many. We all must, in a word, join hands.

Such a situation requires a significant shift in sensibility. It primarily consists of two parts: 1) coming to know the self, and 2) embracing what is "other." Both of these require the development of a viewpoint beyond one's original context.

Knowing the self involves knowing where the self fits and does not fit in the world of selves. In other words, what am I "in on," and what am I "out of?"

It is more likely than not that the person my parents thought I was, is not the person I am. This is true, because my parents were standing in a different context than I was--and consequently saw differently. Further, they will have had psychological reasons for the view they had, and their involvement likely rendered them anything but objective-- whatever that might be.

People around me in my original culture likely could not see me very well as they most likely utilized the viewpoint of that culture, with all its strengths and weaknesses--all its biases and prejudices.

I will likely emerge--to the extent I can ever emerge--from this original culture with the view of myself my parents had, as well as the view my culture had. This will, of course, be one possible view of me, but it may not be very accurate--if by accurate is meant a more complete or well-rounded view.

I may love my original context. I may hate it. I may desire to spend my whole life ensconced in it, or I may desire to get the hell away from it as soon as possible. Why?

This original context will have taught me something about the contexts beyond it. I may have been taught, for example, that the "other" contexts are less than mine, bad, dangerous, &c. I may have been taught they are important, that I should seek them out at all cost.

Just as I need external input to discover who I am, I need external experience to allow me to see my original context with understanding. This requires me to seek difference. It is from the position of difference I will be able to see and begin to understand where I am for the first time.

Then I will know where I *was*. But now the procedure must be repeated, as I now need to know where I am *now*.

The only way I can continue to grow is to seek new contexts and attempt to see from different perspectives. This will require from me a level of openness rather than closure. It may look (especially to insiders) a bit like *Wunderlust,* or even worse: rebellion. One who leaves is often a threat to those who stay, just as one who stays is likely a threat to those who leave.

Is it inevitable we are destined to be threats to each other?

Embracing diversity requires a good deal of self confidence. To feel one is an equal among many demands, among other things, one be able to stand on his or her own feet without constant consensus input from the surround. One must, if you will, know what it means to be Blue and know how to be a Blue in the box with the other Crayons. Here: different is simply different. It is not better or worse.

And one needs to embrace that situation, with it's opportunity for diverse inputs, diverse understanding, and cooperative interactions.

PART II

In light of these considerations, it seems the most important project one has is to discover who one is--and then be that person.

It may seem odd to imagine only some people have a very good sense of who they are. Many people live with the views of themselves they have been taught or the views of who they have imagined themselves to be.

The act of separation and individuation involves breaking away from one's family and the view of one they hold, as well as venturing into the world beyond them in order to find the view one might discover by one's own efforts.

This discovered self will likely retain some elements from one's family as well as combining newer elements as well.

The same will be true of discoveries of the self's culture. Leaving one's culture in order to experience another culture as thoroughly as one can, enables one to see one's original culture in a new light. In this enterprise, strengths and weakness of each may be seen and compared.

Discovering who one is and where one stands in an expanded fashion allows one to be a complete person in life. This is one's gift to life, one's contribution. It is a contribution no other could make.

We are all trying to get into or out of something.

This process suggests a shift in culture. It is a move from a culture of "settling" to a culture that involves significant "moving." The world continually speeds up the opportunity for new experience. Air travel allows for quick coverage of the globe My parents would be stunned by my phone. It makes and receives calls from anywhere I happen to be, takes pictures, plugs into the internet, finds the closest Starbucks, keeps track of appointments, sends and receives messages in three or four different ways, plays movies, and allows me to read books on the bus. It slips into my pocket.

With such portability, I don't need a stable location as much as I did before. Yet I can plug into them. I can keep track of them. And, just as important, I can find maps and directions to new ones as well.

Still, there are times when a stable position is necessary. One is during one's child-rearing years. Children thrive in stable environments and familiar surroundings. It is also the case that most people need to spend a certain portion of their lives working. Few jobs allow wide travel, and wide travel takes one away from one's family.

Further all of us require close friendships and interpersonal connections in order to maintain a healthy measure of well-being and mental health. Someone needs to find us and establish a mutual resonance, or we will get lost. Meaningful connections in both old and new contexts are critical to maximal functioning.

Thus, a life cannot be "all-moving." But the moving part of it has become critical. That is, a life with a stationary period in it is not the same thing as an entire stationary life.

In fact this shift from a modern to a postmodern sensibility is as big a cultural shift as was the shift from religious autocracy to the Renaissance. In other words, we live in a transition culture such as that described in the famous lines from Matthew Arnold (1855):

> Wandering between two worlds,
> one dead,
> The other powerless to be born.

Furthermore, with the speed of development, such a state of transition happens more and more frequently. Even if one does not change location, there are numerous things that change--some dramatically--from year to year.

This insures one's parents were born in a different context from one's own. They may have sought to remain in their original contexts, or they may have been able to readjust and move to newer contexts as these came along. What will their teachings be worth?

Such reasoning does *not* imply everything is relative, in the sense that there is no ground anywhere. Such a (groundless) position ignores the grammar of the language. Grammar remains the ground (Wittgenstein, 1953). A chair for me is the same general sort of thing it was for my parents, though its style may be different. That is to say the grammar of "chair" is the same.

What is likely different is the *ground* upon which we stand to see the chair--the context in which the chair is seen.

Throughout history, according to Foucault (1970), the viewpoints that have prevailed are the one that have been determined by *power*. The use of force and power have stressed viewpoints most favorable to themselves. Reason has either tended to take a back seat in this enterprise or been used in its service.

Such a practice has tended to emphasize and develop a world most amenable to those in power. But such a world has not always been one amenable--or even helpful--to those not in power. Further those not in power vastly outnumber those in power. Thus, we tend to have a world that favors a few. That this continues to be the case is a testimonial to the efficacy of power.

Solutions to this dilemma must be found in order to issue in a world that is able to welcome everyone, *both* the ins and the outs. In short, those outside the influence of power must find a way to aid those trapped within. It will not likely go the other way.

Our lives have become a process of "climbing through" the contexts and influences surrounding us in order to discover and experience newer and different contexts. In this way we are able to grow, and we are able to be part of that segment of culture that is able to grow. This is how the new is able to be dragged out of the culture of the old.

Of course the old tries to preserve itself and puts up resistance. Each step forward is accompanied by equal energy given to steps backward (Freud, 1912/1958). In this light it must be said the old doesn't need to be massacred. It simply needs to be replaced, as one might replace a well worn piece of clothing or leave town for college.

PART III

Organized religion has played a significant role in retarding development over time. This is the case as organized religion has routinely sought power to help it survive. Buber (1948) claimed that whenever the Christian church has had to decide between following its own teachings or grabbing for power, it has unfailingly chosen the latter.

This has been a problem as power typically inheres in the status quo. That is power tends to have power *now*. It is not interested in options to disturb that arrangement by replacing it with something new.

Nonetheless, it may readily be seen that religion has been an important factor in the development of society as we know it. Travels to Italy, if nothing else, indicate what majesty and hope Christianity provided to those who lived in medieval times and who were beset by difficult conditions, illness, and uncertainty. It got them through.

It is also the case that immense numbers of people all over the world exist in largely illiterate conditions. Importantly, these people are able to garner great direction and comfort from their religious experiences.

Religion is not outmoded or useless. But a new opening must be found.

Primitive person found there are things that are deeply meaningful. Birth and death have always been so profound as to garner worship. That there are things that are emotionally meaningful, and deeply so, has always been a part of the human experience. This has been true in addition to the search for knowledge and the expanding of awareness.

While descriptive language has been used in relation to knowledge and understanding, the language of emotion has been metaphor. Here, what is known is used as a springboard to evoke what is felt. "You are a prince," does not mean you are a member of royalty. It means you have shown qualities deserving of royalty. "You are a prince," has an emotional impact beyond saying, "You are a great guy.:

Metaphor, consequently, has been the language of poetry and religion. It evokes what lies beyond simply description.

For example, Saint Matthew (6: 4-13) urged people to avoid churches. He urged them to go home, enter the closet, and pray. And then he suggested a prayer that asks for nothing personal.

But what does "enter the closet" mean? Does this mean: move out the coats and vacuum, enter, and then kneel? Obviously "closet" is here being used as a metaphor. Matthew may well mean "enter yourself," that is enter a region that is private, instead of one that is public--where people largely show off and "already have their reward."

The problem with reading metaphors is they are sometimes not recognized as being metaphors. Then they are assumed to be descriptive elements. "Closet" means "closet." Out with the coats.

As religions become more fundamentalistic, they tend to become more descriptive (the Bible is literally true). As they become more symbolic, they tend to become more metaphorical. A similar situation was suggested by Eliad (1959) in his distinction between the sacred and the profane.

Metaphorical focus in religion tends toward an experience. Descriptive focus tends toward dogma. It may be said there is a difference between the experience of the sacred and the following of dogma. As my brother (laughingly) says: "Dogma is left-brain, whereas the sacred is right brain."

The point is that following dogma and experiencing the sacred are really two very different kinds of things. Dogma religion tends to be profane. Sacred religion is....wait for it....sacred.

Religion in our time has basically tended toward dogma. We stand up and then sit down, over and over, at Mass. Why is that important? We pray on time, according to set schedules. We bow toward Mecca.

Almost universally this dogma requires *compliance*. There are consequences if one does not comply. In such an environment, compliance quickly becomes the focal point. One's devotion is measured by it, along with one's standing.

Clearly prior generations could abide such regulations. As time has progressed, however, the requirement to comply with something external to one's experienced truth has increasingly become a problem.

Placing oneself in a strict exoskeleton may seem desirable to one who has an inadequate endoskeleton, but it is not a process of interest to a more healthy personality.

One who has struggled to become aware of his or her self has likely done so for the purpose of being able to live his or her own genuine life-- make one's own genuine contribution. By crippling this healthy self by putting it in a corset of external rules and judgments (and therefore changing it), one does not make progress. This is especially true if the rules and judgments were developed centuries before when the world was a dramatically different place.

Still, part of the human experience is to find some things meaningful. It is also part of that experience to find some things so meaningful they can be said to be sacred to one. The love one has for one's child is an example.

So what is to be done with this "sacred" part?

Clearly there is no reason to follow dogma in order to experience the sacred. Anyone with a developed emotional or metaphorical ability can do it. And it doesn't require a church or "official" place either. It can happen along a sidewalk. Even Sixth Avenue.

And it doesn't matter what it is called. God. The transcendent. Heaven. Father. Mother. The Great Spirit. The eternal. Time. Even the "windowless monad."

It is the experience of placing oneself in accord with that which is greater than one is. And it can be different for everyone. There are no rules and no requirements. There is only the truth of one's experience from the center of one's true self.

This is to place all elements in accord. This is to allow life to function at its fullest. And it is to stop baring one of the most significant experiences from legions who do not wish to join organizations and conform.

Religion, as we now know it, is routinely in the way of that enterprise, whereas the profound experience of the sacred facilitates it.

REFERENCES

Arnold, M. "Stanzas from the Grande Chartreuse," in The Norton Anthology of English Literature. Vol. 2. Norton. 1968, pp. 1040-1045.

Buber, M. Tales of the Hasidim: Later Masters. Schocken. 1948.

Campbell, J. The Inner Reaches of Outer Space: Metaphor and Myth and as Religion. Harper. 1986.

Campbell, J. Transformations of Myth Through Time. Harper Perennial, 1999.

Eliad, M. Myth and Reality. Harper. 1963.

Eliad M. The Sacred and the Profane: The Nature of Religion. Harcourt. 1959.

Foucault, M. The Order of Things: An Archaeology of the Human Sciences. Random House. 1970.

Freud, S. The Dynamics of Transference (1912), in The Standard Edition of the Complete Psychological Works of Sigmund Freud, Vol 12. Trans J. Strachey. Hogarth. 1958, pp. 97-108.

Rilke, R.M. The Notebooks of Malte Laurids Brigge. Trans. M.D.H. Norton. Norton. 1949.

Wittgrenstein, L. Philosophical Investigations. Trans. G.E.M. Anscombe. Macmillan, 1953.

GENDER

Alice laughed. "There's no use trying," she said: "one *ca'n't* believe impossible things."

"I daresay you haven't had much practice," said the Queen. "When I was your age I always did it for half-an-hour a day. Why, sometimes I've believed as many as six impossible things before breakfast.

--Lewis Carroll
Through the Looking Glass

"Right answers" run into trouble with the realization that what one sees depends upon where one stands. Then there are many "right answers." Grasping these new views requires a kind of comprehension-mobility. The exclusion of viewpoints, long routine, is not, intellectually at least, an aid to understanding.

Both pre-modern to modern times tended to ignore or downplay the legitimate concerns of women and others who were routinely considered ancillary to a patriarchal point of view. The direct consideration of women and excluded voices has received more direct focus in the post-modern period. One place where this comes to light most clearly is in considerations involving gender.

Klages (1997) argued that topics like gender and also race come to focus when cultures or understood "roles" are undergoing change. Further, she noted gender roles have shifted in practically every period.

She said:

Certainly in the nineteenth century (my field of expertise), in Britain and the United States, gender was a matter for much public discussion and debate. "The Woman Question," as it was called, focused on whether gender should be a factor in granting or limiting rights, like voting rights; it also focused attention on men and male social nature and function of gender. Is gender innate and biological? Is it the product of socialization and environment? Is the family structure (one father, one mother, and kids) eternal, universal, divinely-ordained, natural--or socially constructed and thus variable? These were--and are—central questions, not only for politics and economics, but for anthropology, psychology, and all of what we now call the social sciences.

Gender is universal. Everywhere and at all times there has been an issue of different distinctions for the sexes (vaguely defined). Typically power issues and anatomy have drawn the distinctions, and little beyond was considered. In our time, however, we have had our linguistic considerations heightened, and we think of gender as a construction (see Derrida, 1974).

(From Wittgenstein (1953) we learned "gender" is a *word* grammatically related to "language games" that have a "family resemblance.")

This alone is a huge shift in sensibility. What used to be an "obvious truth or fact" has become instead a cultural construction. This, of course, raises the question: "Why construct things that way?" "What are the implications of such a construction?"

According to postmodernism, constructions in the first place are dependent upon language for their understanding.

Postmodernists argue that thought is irreducibly linguistic; it can be practiced only in and through historyical and context-dependent "language games" or "discourses"... There is no reality for us outside such systems because, as Rorty argues, "there is no way to think about either the world or our purposes except by using language"... All language games generate their own rules about how to play, what counts as a successful move, and so forth. But by definition these rules are context dependent and valid only within a particular game. Games and their rules are incommensurable (Flax, 1990, p. 202).

Foucault (1994), for example, undertook his study "An Archaeology of the Human Sciences." He looked at scientific papers from the past several eras. What he found was scarcely an objective undertaking. He found instead the questions asked, the experiments conceived, the data considered, and the interpretation of those data were each heavily influenced by the times and the cultural conditions during which such experiments took place. Thus, social issues influenced what was thought, discovered, and understood--that is, what was constructed.

This kind of study ushered in postmodernism and also drove a nail in notions of universal truths and essential certainties. It meant what one saw was importantly colored by where one stood.

An example of this in terms of the study of gender was offered by Fausto-Sterling (2000). (Dr. Fausto-Sterling is a research biologist at Brown University.)

Individual scientists are inclined to believe one or another claim about biology based in part on scientific evidence and in part on whether the claim confirms some aspects of life that seems personally familiar...[for example] labeling someone a man or a woman is a social decision. We may use scientific knowledge to help us make the decision, but only our beliefs about gender—not science—can define our sex. Furthermore, our beliefs about gender affect what kinds of knowledge scientists produce about sex in the first place...*Our bodies are too complex to provide clear-cut answers about sexual difference.* The more we look for a simple physical basis for "sex," the more it becomes clear that "sex" is not a pure physical category. What bodily signals and functions we define as male or female come already entangled in our ideas about gender (pp. ix, 4, and 5). (My italics.)

Thus: *what I see and know is constructed from what I am able to find and is carried in the language I am able to use.*

The constructs that come to be commonly accepted at any time and in any place are more the result of the operations of power [authority] than they are of accuracy or "truth."

I construct a sense of myself in the interpersonal context of my family, all members of which have their own constructs of me. Thus my construction is influenced by its context.

When I seek a therapist, I meet with a person who seeks to develop his or her own construct of me—hopefully based on some theoretical understanding (itself a construct). He or she will then attempt to learn about my own construct of myself. We will develop constructs of each other—and of the relationship we have created and maintain (the "analytic third").

Still, hopefully in there somewhere, we will both find ways to construct things differently. This gives us a chance to experience things differently and hopefully to discover a more workable world in which to function—as well as a more effective construct of self.

Let us now consider a group of words and their grammar that *accomplish* something. The classic example is this: If I utter the words 'I do' in the right place and at the right time, I have not described something, I have *married someone*. That is, the utterance of such words in the designated situation *performs* the act of marrying. These linguistic elements are called "performative utterances (Austin, 1961)."

Austin said:

> ...if a person makes an utterance
> of this sort we should say that he is
> *doing* something rather than merely *saying* something (p. 222).

In a sense, *performative* utterances are ways of "doing things with words."

Now consider the same logic applied to behavior. Some behaviors may be seen as accomplishing something. For example, waving in the right context signals "good-by." In a different context the same behavior signals "hello."

If I sit with another in a room and behave according to specific principles, I can be said to be "doing psychotherapy," &c.

Several contemporary thinkers (e.g. Butler, 1991, 1993, Goldner, 2002) have suggested that to a great extent gender is performative.

Butler's (Ibid) example was "drag." If I am a certain sort of person and I wear a certain kind of clothes, and embellish them in a certain kind of way, I may be said to be "in drag." That is, my doing those things is what makes it drag.

Another sort of person doing similar things may not be doing drag but may just be doing "Godawful."

Klages (1997) made the following observations:

> Butler looks at how Freud tells thestory of how fantasy identifications (identifications that happen in the unconscious) shape our identity (who we are). When we identify with someone else, we create an internal image [i.e., "notion"] of that person, or, more precisely, who we want that person to be, and then we identify

with that internalized and idealized image. Our own identity,
then, isn't modeled on actual others but on our image of their image, on what we want the other to
be, rather than what the other really is.

Gender, then, as the identification with one sex,
or one object (like the mother) is a fantasy, a set of
internalized images, and not a set of properties
governed by the body and its organ configuration.
Rather, gender is a set of signs internalized, psy-
chically imposed on the body and on one's psychic
sense of identity. Gender, Butler concludes, is thus
not a primary category, but an attribute, a set of
secondary narrative effects.

Gender is thus a fantasy enacted by "corporeal
styles that constitute bodily significations." In other words, gender is an act, a performance, a set of
manipulated codes, costumes, rather than a core
aspect of essential identity. Butler's main metaphor
for this is "drag," i.e. dressing like a person of the
"opposite sex." All gender is a form of "drag," ac-

cording to Butler; there is no "real" core gender to refer to.

This point is made with searing clarity by Wilchins (1997) as Butler's notions apply to queer culture and the specific issue of transgender individuals:

> The unstructured multiplicity, the sheer creativity of queer genders strike at the very foundations of heterosexuality, and this is exactly why queers have historically been targets for straight prejudice, bashing, and outright hatred...You say we [transgender persons] want to "pass" [be taken as] women. Well, I don't pass. I wear this Transsexual Menace logo every place I go. Between the two of us, only you pass as a woman. If, as Beauvoir held, "One is not born a woman, but becomes one," if femininity is an invention of man foisted on women, if feminine behavior is a learned cultural performance of

hair, clothing, voice, gesture, and stance so one is perceived as a female, then by presenting yourself as a woman it is you who have been co-opted into traditional sex roles, you who serve their institutions, and you who are performing here (p. 61).

In similar fashion Goldner (2002) argued "society demands of one a gendered self." This cannot *not* be done. Further, in our culture there are two options: male and female. The question for her was how do we come to be accepted as a member of each group? Her answer is we must be taught to do some things and not others. It would not work (i.e., be sufficiently distinguishing) if we were to just do what we want, what we "feel like" doing--as we would do too many of the same things.

Further the main task we have, according to her, is the *suppression of similarities*. The way we walk must be different, the way we sit, the clothes we wear. In short the *difference* between us is critical.   Diman (2002) goes even farther and suggests the point of gender is to "create difference."

So why do we do it? Why do we contort ourselves so in pursuit of artifice—and further in pursuit of an artifice we would not pursue without social pressure to do so? Goldner (Ibid) felt that the culture desires the split in genders as it reinforces the male power hegemony. That is, culturally, the male artifice is considered to have more power than the female artifice.

Goldner's thoughts stem from the contemporary context in which Enlightenment principles such as universal truth, beauty, justice, power, &c. are seen to gloss critical individual differences. Further, enlightenment principles directly fueled "colonialism," in which one group who claimed the truth overpowered and assimilated other groups. In a way men "colonialised" women. Alterity prevailed.

Finally, for those groups who have always been and still are Other or marginal to the constructed history of European civilization, we both do and do not participate in the heritage of the Enlightenment. Because [for example] women's role in the history of the European Enlightenment and in the literary and artistic history of Modernism is so severely limited, I am outside it, always Other, always not included. Because the roles of Jews and Gypsies in that history are likewise limited, I am outside it also as a Jew and a non-ethnic Gypsy. It both was and was not my Enlightenment. I stand in this intellectual history with a double and divided consciousness...because it erased me, it is not and never was my Enlightenment (Johnson, 2004.)

Unlike before, the current period is able to see things like gender from a perspective that includes the notion of the unconscious and its (unrealized) impact on our "objectivity." We are able to see the critical importance of relationships and interpersonal empathy beyond simply relying on reason/power and "objective" (empirical) enterprises. We see the need to hear from diverse sources instead of experts to broaden our arena of consideration. And we realize the central role of language in the construction of our understanding of reality.

Currently we are seen as inescapably entwined in our (specific) cultural contexts in terms of what we can imagine, study, think about, experience, &c. That is, the Enlightenment notions of finding universal objective, rational, scientifically based truths that are "eternally true" is simply not possible from our perspective. No thinking, no science, no "reason," no cultural principles have been able to completely transcend their context. Thus, as in ordinary language, it is the context—not the object—that most often determines that object's meaning and significance (see Foucault, 1994, Wittgenstein, 1953, et.al).

Monique Witting has observed that "...the first, the permanent, and the final social contract is language." Our bodies—as signs in that language—are the first and most permanent ele-ment of that linguistic contract, and in order to participate in the social space of language, we agree to be our "selves" as we are seen by others, that is, our particular physical selves—fat or thin, black or white, young or old. The most basic part of that linguistic contract to which our bodies are apprenticed is to be sexed, and being sexed in this context does not mean agreeing to mouth the words "I am female," to answer to the name, or to mark box next to *Male* with an *X*. It means agreeing to feel and look and act your sex, to participate in society as a meaningful member within the matrix of expectations that go along with your sex (Wilchins, pp 133, 134).

This point, stressed by Butler (2004), underscores the unconscious shaping of our thoughts by having been required to conform to cultural and familial norms--instead of being encouraged to be who we are. This is why the struggle to discover the shards of who we are behind such training is a central part of substantial psychotherapy and psychoanalysis.

The search for fundamental truths has been replaced by attempts to destabilize general, fundamental, essential concepts and replace them with a collection of particular, context dependent—and even uncertain—observations and linguistic constructions.

This comment suggests major differences between women and men are largely the result of cultural patterns instead of the result of anatomical differences between them.

Goldner (2002) held:

> Women's sexuality (*contra* Freud) is *never* truly phallic/genital. Unlike the man's, the woman's pleasure is never centered on one organ or orient-ed to one aim: orgasmic (tension) release. Rather, it is plural: "Woman has sex organs more or less everywhere...the geography of

her pleasure is far more diversified, more multiple in its differences, more complex, more subtle, than is commonly imagined...This fluid and unbounded female sexuality cannot be conceptualized within masculine parameters (pp. 75-76).

The function of binary labor divisions, it is argued (Goldner, 2002), is to perpetuate the patriarchal advantage. Such a system encourages males to operate in the "outside world" and compete for honors, whereas it encourages women to stay home where they are largely "out of sight" with children (rarely do the media or popular attention, for example, cover "at home" experiences with the vigor or depth in which "out in the world" experiences are covered—unless, that is, they are attempting to "lure" women away from careers and back to their homes in the service of the patriarchal tradition [see Faludi, 1992].)

Cutting edge theorists in our time have suggested the elimination of the concept of gender altogether. Butler (2004), for example, spoke about conceptions "Beyond Gender." Goldner (2000)

argued gender is a social role and a social pro-
scription required to maintain current power positions. Further these social roles are attained to the
satisfaction of social constructs by suppressing
elements of our common humanity.

Goldner argued:

> Moreover, with regard to gender
> injunctions, the child is being put
> in an untenable position merely
> because of his or her sex. Since it
> is the arbitrary fact of the child's
> sex, not anything particular to the
> child's [individual] person, that
> prompts the parent to demand or
> expect compliance and understand-
> ing, gender is being infused with
> powerful, polarizing, relational
> meanings that the child, perforce,
> internalizes into his or her identity
> structure. Indeed, in my view, it is
> these overdetermined, internally
> contradictory, deeply embedded
> relationship premises that are al-

ways at risk of collapsing under
their own weight that constitute the
pathogenic, wobbly bedrock of
gender (Ibid. p. 84).

It is the internalization of such family constella-
tions and one's place in them that results in pathological formations.

Since complying with contradicto-
ry gender injunctions and reifica-
tions is tied to sustaining the
child's primary object relations [re-
lationship with his or her parents],
the child must accommodate to
these impossible terms by performing acts of internal violence on the
self. In so doing, the relational
complexity of the internal world
fragments, and ambivalence de-
volves into splitting and false-self
operations (Ibid, p. 85).

Thus society demands of one a gendered self. In order to learn a gender to the satisfaction of one's peers, one primarily must *suppress* one's similarities with the differing gender. Thus one must learn *to plausibly perform a role.* Further, there are two roles and identity structures from which one might choose. In this way, each person is distorted from the kind of being he or she might be if not required to follow these "social scripts." In other words gender training requires a splitting in personal identity. It frequently also requires projection, projective identification, reaction formation, and a perpetual "false self."

De Beauvoir (1949) stressed women are considered "lesser" to men. This is not due to anything in her "essence" but by social construction. Further, women bear the responsibility of their own transformation, as well as the transformation of society, despite the fact they have been long trained to be timid, passive, modest, and to act in "bad faith."

Benjamin (1988) also argued that anything other than an open, empathic resonance between persons involves domination. This means someone is being erased. If I dominate you, I erase you. If you dominate me, you erase me.

Further both men and women are shaped and influenced by changing notions about gender. We are taught how to be. Thus there are ways we could get it wrong. The further assumption here is that persons within each the male and female groups are actually *like* each other--enough to form a sensible grouping ("women are somehow like "women," and "men" are somehow like "men"). This is to say that in-group variance is largely elided in the service of group maintenance.

Deviations from "approved" group inclusion is routinely discouraged if not punished. We *need* this difference. "Deviations" in this area are among the least tolerated. The use of force is routine. Weber (1958) argued the rule of law is not dissevered from force and violence.

Nonetheless, gender relations form a central element in the construction of a sense of self. In this regard truths of biological sex have been transformed into gender notions.

Rubin (1975) argued:

..sex as we know it--gender identity, sexual desire and fantasies, concepts of childhood--is itself a social
product.

Clearly notions of gender are social constructions. For example, an essential element in the
construction of gender is the division of labor
along sexual lines. This construction continues to
function as a taboo that reinforces separateness.

As Goldner argued above, gender is not a natural
outgrowth or consequence of biology. Rather it is
the result of sanctions against displays of similarity between sexes.

Further, according to Rubin, the family is the
chief agent in the socialization of women. Families are routinely constituted with men as the power element and women as subservient. Thus, this
is a case of men who dominate and women who
submit. In such a system, women are not allowed
to be themselves lest they threaten the power bal-
ance (see also Chodorow, 1978).

The first "other" we experience and rely on is likely to have been a woman. The critical importance of this experience in our developmental sequence is hard to over-stress. In fact, when it comes to basic human well-being and functioning, a loving, empathic foundation is the greatest gift possible.

Chodorow (Ibid.) focused specifically on the phenomenon of "motherhood." In her view the experience of the newborn is a combination of rapture due to the love, warmth, and care he or she receives from the mother. But it also includes terror at the experience of dependence. How this equation is handled in the mother child dyad has critical implications for future sexual relations of the child. Specifically, failure in this experience can lead to unconscious rage as well as a need to control.

Thus it is from our mothers and our attachment experiences with them we learn our sense of what it is to be a human being.

According to Chodorow, the identification of little girls and motherhood as well as the avoidance of intimacy and female identification in little

boys is not the result of nature or biological processes. They are, on the other hand, the product of
social considerations surrounding the social construction of families--and are reinforced by relations with others within the family (which, of
course, is an entity maintained within broader social relations and structures).

Thus infantile experiences of role performance
figure importantly in notions of gender, the division of labor, and what is "domestic" versus what
is "public."

The following sequence ensues. Infants are attended by mothers who have some view of the infant: who he or she is, what his or her life will
likely be, is he or she like me, not like me, &c.
Mothers also have relationships with fathers. This
is warm and mutual, cold and distant, deeply con-
flicted, remarkably equal, &c.

The parents tell the child who he or she is, how
important he or she is, how welcome, how much
trouble, &c. These experiences profoundly influence the child's developing sense of self. Parents'
notions of gender, their own and the child's, as

well as avenues available for such a child become highly influential.

Around eighteen months to two years of life, the infant discovers he or she and the mother are *separate beings*. That is, enough grammar has been learned that the child has the tools to separate things. This realization issues in the first tragedy of life: I could have a need, and mother, being apart, might not know it. With this realization the edifice of infantile narcissism shatters, and the child feels alone.

How this is handled is critical. It might be okay if loving people surround me, people who are able to empathically respond to my concerns. If, on the other hand, my parents are cold, self absorbed, or distancing, I will likely be overwhelmed and feel apart in a frightening world.

The next question is: since I am a separate person, what *kind* of separate person am I? If I am a daughter, I can learn I am a person who is like my mother, even if I am a separate creature. (Routinely my mother also reinforces this similarity.) If I am a son, however, I must learn *mother is other*. Thus I have to suppress my identification with my mother and join up with those like my father. As Butler (2002) argued, however, I am going to suppress my identification with *which* mother? Will this be the external mother? That task is (almost) doable. But what about the internalized mother? I've got that one inside with me. *Fait accompli.*

My only choice is to suppress this inner mother as best I can and struggle with all my might to make sure I don't display any mother (feminine) traits. And...I have to avoid women. Being close with women brings up the internal identification with my mother I am trying to suppress and is threatening. Treating women as objects also helps.

If all goes well, my sister and I appear to be very different creatures when we are three or four years old. And my parents tell everyone we have always been that way--even though we were raised *"identically."*

Obviously when this pattern is minimized, children are freer to be who they are. The daughter doesn't have to be like the mother, and the son doesn't have to distort and hide half of himself. To accomplish this, however, the family has to be set up differently from the "typical" family so many of us have known. My parents have to be more interested in who I am than they are in requiring me fit some social notion.

Again, it is the power of the parents, as agents of the larger social order, that allows me to maximize myself or molds me to culturally defined stereotypes. These stereotypes, further, have little to do with me--as a unique individual.

When I become a parent, I become a power-broker, whether or not I like it. What stereotype wishes do I have for my child? Can I really empathically join with him or her and listen? And if I do what will this mean for the intense social shaping of school? There, the issue of who the child really is may never be addressed. The focus will be on adjusting and achieving.

Suffice it to say, one's social role will play a significant part in one's life. Will I be able to meld my real self and at least enough of an approved social self to survive as a real person--as who I am?

This issue becomes more acute when sub-cultures are addressed. These exist due to location, income brackets, race, age, religious issues, &c. Clearly, sub-groups do not all have the same notions, experiences, opportunities, &c. If each voice is to be heard, sub-group voices in their multi-dimensional individuality must be heard. All of them.

Even so, in too many parts of the world gross anatomy sentences one to a life that cannot properly be called *human*.

The multiplicity of experiences and training leads one to imagine a *fluid conception of gender*. That is, gender is not one thing, and certainly it is not always the same thing. Gender roles vary widely within gender identities. Gender identities themselves are more or less reflective of individuals and cultural notions involved. There is no essential thing all women have in common, nor is there an essential thing all men have in common. It simply is not that simple.

We can think in terms of the "given" and the "made." The given is some phenomenon that exists, and the made is how we interpret it--what significance it has for us. Thus there are the people in the world, and there is how we think about them. In this regard, gender is a "made." It is how we think about people--what, for example, qualities we attribute to them.

Goldner (2002) suggested these notions come into clear view when a child is born with ambiguous genitalia. Such a phenomenon challenges the accepted gender binary. And it is a measure of the importance we place on gender stability that such a situation raises an issue that demands immediate resolution. Further, there are only two possibilities: this or that. That the child may already be in a unique or third sort of category is routinely not considered.

Biological data are collected, notions of the possibility of "successful" gender operation are considered, and the child is *assigned* to a group.

If you think about it, we are all assigned to a group in similar fashion. Our culture, the school system, our dress codes, &c. will tolerate little else. This is a game that *must* be played. It must be played, that is, unless we find our genuine selves and can realize them away from, or in addition to, the cultural false-self that is required.

Or we can become gender-odd and basically ignore or flout the cultural notions.

It is further interesting that such binary assignment differs so widely from our other notions of individual difference. That is we know physical traits like height, weight, I.Q. scores, axon myelinization, &c. are normally distributed. But this is not how we consider gender. No. Gender is either totally skinny or totally fat. Black or white. Gender, in other words, is a *borderline* condition.

Our data suggest otherwise. Gender too is normally distributed. No two of us look alike.

Enlightenment notions failed because all men do not seem to be created equal. Some have advantages others simply do not. Gender notions fail for similar reasons. That is, we are assigned to categories that don't always (ever?) fit.

The cost in this is too great. It seems we have come to a point in our development where notions of gender and gender training have too often become an impediment to genuine, individual self realization and expression. That is, who we are as a person is more important than whether we are equal, male or female, in power or not, rich or poor, &c.

Were we all to "come clean" tomorrow and expose ourselves as exactly who we know ourselves to be, what would be the down-side? First of all we would have to change some of our concepts. Our assumptions. What would we lose if we assumed each of us were basically *persons*? We look different. We live in different biases and places. We have been taught different stuff. We are, in short, a rainbow--and we *can* all be accommodated.

It *will* change the power equation.

And it *needs* to change the power equation.

When power destroys talent, human potential, tenderness, and human compassion, it has become a liability to humanity. We are better being who we are than who we have been required to be.

REFERENCES

Austin, J.L. "Performative Utterances" in Austin, J.L. Philosophical Papers, (Eds.) Urmson, J.O., and Warnock, G.J. Oxford. 1961. Pp 220-239.

Benjamin J. The Bonds of Love: psychoanalysis, feminism, and the problem of domination. Pantheon, 1988.

Benjamin, J. Like Subjects, Love Objects: essays on recognition and sexual difference. Yale, 1995.

Buber, M. Tales of the Hasidim: Later Masters. Schoken. 1948.

Butler, J. Gender Trouble, Routledge, 1999.

Butler, J. "Melancholy Gender-Refused Identification." In Gender In Psychoanalytic Space: between clinic and culture. (Eds.) M. Dimen, and V. Goldner. Other, 2002.

Butler, J. Undoing Gender. Routledge, 2004.

Chodorow, N.J. Feminism and Psychoanalytic Theory. Yale. 1989.

de Beauvoir, S. The Second Sex. Bantam. 1961.

Derrida, J. Of Grammatology, Corrected Edition. Hopkins, 1974.

Diman, M. "Deconstructing Difference: Gender, Splitting, and Transitional Space." In (Eds.) Diman, M., and Goldner, V. Gender in Psychoanalytic Space: Between Clinic and Culture. Other Press, 2002

Dinnerstein, D. The Mermaid and the Minotaur: Sexual Arrangements and the Human Malaise. Harper. 1976.

Faludi, S. Backlash: the Undeclared War Against American Women. Anchor. 1991.

Fausto-Sterling, A. Sexing the Body: gender politics and the sexing of the body. Basic, 2000.

Flax, J.   Thinking Fragments: psychoanalysis, feminism, and postmodernism in the contemporary west. California, 1990.

Foucault, M. The Order of Things: an archeology of the human sciences. Vintage, 1994.

Goldner, V."Toward a Critical Relational Theory of Gender," in Gender in Psychoanalytic Space: between clinic and culture. (Eds.) M. Dimen and V. Goldner. Other, 2002.

Irigaray, L. This Sex Which is not One. (Trans.) C. Porter. Cornell. 1985.

Irigaray, L.   "Speculum of the Other Woman. (Trans.) G.C. Gill. Cornell. 1985.

Johnson, 2004.

Klages, M.   http://www.colorado.edu/English/ courses/ENGL2012Klages/butler.html 1997.

Klages, M.   http://www.colorado.edu/English/ courses/ENGL2012Klages/pomo.html 2003.

Rorty, R. "Pragmatism," in Bayes, K., Bohman, and McCarthty, T. After Philosophy: End or Transformation? MIT, 1978.

Rubin, G. "The Traffic in Women: Notes on the 'Political Economy' of Sex," in Toward an Anthropology of Women. (Ed.) R.R. Ritter. Monthly Review Press. 1975.

Wilchins, R.A. Read My Lips: Sexual Subversion and the End of Gender. Firebrand. 1997.

Wittgenstein, L. Philosophical Investigations. (Trans.) G.E.M. Anscombe. Macmillan, 1953.

(1) The more one reads about contemporary thought and sensibility it is astonishing how often the crux of the problem at issue has to do with power. Perhaps it is the so-called masculine way of doing things. If it isn't religion that preaches love while it grabs power and dictates rules and regulations to be followed, it is parents who treat their children as not-yet-citizens and therefore not

yet to be considered seriously on their own terms--
or the need of students to figure how to please
narcissistic professors instead of speaking their
own minds. Experts and authorities seem to be
everywhere.

LITTLE MYTHS AND STORIES

For the new locus is never
Hidden inside the old one
Where Reason could rout it out,
Nor guarded by dragons in distant
Mountains where Imagination
Could explore it; the place of birth
It is too obvious and near to notice,
Some dull dogpatch a stone's throw
Outside the walls, reserved
For the eyes of faith to find.

-- W.H. Auden
The Age of Reason

An essential experience of human beings is to grapple with comprehension. And it is clear comprehension is not only intellectually based. Just as primitive persons feared creatures they felt lurked in the mist, so we too fear dangers in what we cannot see. It might be said there has been a tremendous effort over the centuries to penetrate the mist and push back the area of unknown darkness.

It is not always, and has not always been, easy going. Numerous conscious and unconscious ideas, beliefs, patterns, localisms, one-sided views, prejudices, &c. stand in the way. And in no small way, this progress has been movement from a world largely comprised of beliefs to a world more largely comprised of realities--both physical and emotional.

Bastian (See Kopping, 2005) made a distinction between what he called "elementary ideas" (*Elementargedanken*) and cultural or "folk ideas" (*Volkergedanken*). His notion is somewhat similar to Plato's distinction between "universals" and "particulars."

Consider, for example, the concept: beauty. Beauty is an elementary idea, a universal, as it is a concept that exists in all different cultures and areas. There is always something beautiful. On the other hand, exactly what culture X holds to be beautiful (e.g., nose studs) is particular to that culture and is therefore a folk idea.

Thus each culture may have a different version of what is beautiful, but each has the notion of beauty.

This is how many religions operate. There is, say, always something held to be sacred. Just what that is in culture or religion Y, however, is likely to be different from what it is in culture or religion Z. What is fashionable in New York City is different from what is fashionable in Mississippi, Denver, or Los Angeles--not to mention Rome or Riyadh.

Bastian's distinction, however, differs from that of Plato in that he is trying to distinguish between notions of, say, eternal truths and, say, social perceptions and norms. Thus questions of the nature of the essence of what is human in the universe differ from how we manage traffic intersections in our country or "what we value most" around here.

In a similar way mythologies can be cosmological or they can be local. Myths and stories about cosmic structure may be called big myths and stories. Myths and stories about the way things are locally may be called little myths and stories.

Any of these are susceptible to being believed and treated as truths. Thus we may believe a story. We may live in terms of it. We may feel it pertains in some special way to our lives.

Metaphor is common in these myths and stories and is the grammatical device that allows us to reach beyond the physical facts in front of us in order to add an additional dimension.

Chaos results when metaphorical statements are taken as descriptive facts. In such cases the closure of the metaphorical opening erases contact with the world beyond.

Campbell (1986), for example, spoke about the notion that "Jesus, having risen from the dead, ascended physically to heaven (Luke 24:51), to be followed shortly by his mother in her sleep...It is also written that some nine centuries earlier, Elijah, riding a chariot of fire, had been carried to heaven in a whirlwind (2 Kings 2:11)" (p. 30).

Obviously, if anything of value is to be made of [these ideas] at all (and I submit that the elementary original idea must have been something of this kind), where those bodies went was not into outer space, but into inner space. That is to say, what is connoted by such metaphorical voyages is the possibility of a return of the mind in spirit, while still incarnate, to full knowledge of that transcendent source out of which the mystery of a given life arises into this field of time and back into which it in time dissolves (p. 31)

Campbell pointed out that if, on the other hand, these three were traveling at the speed of light, they "would not yet be out of the galaxy."

Art uses the same metaphorical devices to open us to something beyond the physical--to the mystery and majesty of what lies beyond.

Yet moving beyond the physical and the immediate has not always been considered to be of value. Almost from the beginning there have been attempts to move religion, for example, from a direct experience of the transcendent divine to a dutiful obedience of a set of rules--that is something the metaphorically-challenged could comprehend.

In this way, the connotation of the metaphor is sealed off, and the only thing left is the physical.

Zoroaster (see Zoroaster), for example, suggested a theology radically different from the attempt to put oneself in accord with the transcendent rhythms. For Zoroaster the goal was not, say, mystical union with the divine, but to take sides with the forces of light (good) against the forces of darkness (evil).

Here the mythology becomes one of proper conduct instead of an opening to the world beyond. It is a mythology that takes place entirely on the physical plane.

The "one against another" or "us-them" split is clearly seen in this following passage Campbell (1986) cited from Deuteronomy:

> When you draw near to a city to fight against it, offer terms of peace to it. And if its answer to you is peace and it opens to you, then all the people who are found in it shall do forced labor for you and shall serve you. But if it makes no peace with you, but makes war against you, then you shall besiege it; and when the Lord your God gives it into your hand you shall put all its males to the sword, but the women and little ones, the cattle, and everything else in the city, all its spoil, you shall take a booty for yourselves, and you shall enjoy

the spoil of your enemies, which the Lord your God has given you. Thus you shall do to all the cities which are very far from you, which are not cities of the nations here. But in the cities of these people that the Lord your God gives you for an inheritance, you shall save alive nothing that breathes, but you shall utterly destroy them...as the Lord your God has commanded. (Deuteronomy 20: 10-18).

Clearly the plane has shifted to the mere physical. But other elements have appeared as well. First is the astounding lack of empathy or any sense of mentalization (awareness that in dealing with another, I am dealing with a person who has thoughts and feelings just as I have, see Fonagy, 1998). In the above example, the "bad guys" are to be treated as objects. And further this is made *proper*.

Second is the use of a myth or story to define and control. It is our culture versus theirs--may the best culture win. It is virtually a proclamation of alterity.

Campbell said:

> So that one of the first concerns of the elders, prophets, and established priesthoods of tribal or institution-ally oriented mythological systems has always been to limit and define the permitted field of expression of this expansive faculty of the heart [metaphor], holding it to a fixed focus within the field exclusively of the ethnic monad, while deliberately directing outward every impulse to violence (Ibid, p. 16)

In this view the cultural focus of myths is not to open the mind and heart, but on the contrary to bind these capacities to the local group--as well as defining such narrowing as the pursuit of the good.

The Mormons, for example, say of their restrictions that they follow a "higher standard."

They also encourage their children to be "in the world but not of the world."

Such practices could be called the literalization of myths in the service of group versus group instead of the opening of hearts and minds to the region "beyond things" or the notion of all groups bonding together in a larger (human) group. The important Zen notion of one hand clapping--that is the region beyond the physical where things don't run into each other--becomes simply gibberish.

The power of such (little) myths and stories creeps into and colors how the world and things are seen from points of view in such a way they are difficult to detect. A well-traveled friend told me that if you travel in Russia, the most impressive buildings are the buildings of State; if you travel in Western Europe, the most impressive buildings are the churches; if you travel in the United States, the most impressive buildings are the banks.

Also in the United States there are the notions of "mother, home, apple pie, the stars and stripes, &c." These are images of a wholesome people--people, furthermore, who came from a wholesome beginning. Residents can "participate" in this characterization and feel good about themselves. And it may remain uncritically examined.

Russell (2010) presents a different view.

Many, and probably most, inhabitants of early American cities were corrupt and depraved, and the founding Fathers knew it. Alexander Hamilton called the behaviors of Americans "vicious" and "vile." Samuel Adams saw a "torrent of vice" running through the new country. John Jay wrote of his fear that "our conduct should confirm to tory maxim 'that men are incapable of governing themselves.'" James Warren, the president of the Provincial Congress of Massachusetts and a Paymaster General of the Continental army, declared during the Revolution that Americans lived "degenerate days." As the war with the British thundered on, John Adams grew so disgusted at what he saw on the streets that at times he believed Americans deserved death more than freedom. Their dissolute character "is enough to induce every Man of Sense and Virtue to abandon such an execrable Race, to their own Perdition, and if they could be ruined alone it would be just."...And in the fall of that year when British forces under General Howe appeared poised to invade Philadelphia, John Adams told his wife of his secret wish for the revolutionary capital to be captured by the British, for it "would cure Americans of their vicious and luxurious and effeminate Appetites, Passions and Habits" (Russell, 2010, pp 3,4,28).

In accounts such as this the "good guys" begin to lose their savor and patina. In fact they begin to resemble pious monsters. (Think of the sermons of Jonathan Edwards.) We begin cheering for the open space and light earned for us by the "bad guys."

This influence of notions carried in local myths and stories is akin to Wittgenstein's (1953) notion of "pictures."

> A picture held us captive, and we could not get outside it, for it lay in our language, and language seemed to repeat it to us inexorably (PI 115).

The issue is it does not occur to us to question these myths, stories, and pictures. They, if you can stand it, lie in our culture and are repeated endlessly.

The American president Ronald Reagan generated the notion that small government is better than big government. This idea took hold and attained somewhat of a mythical status. Without examination certain people take this view to be the case.

Such things can happen as language is used for much more than simply stating facts. Some language is used to influence. It is being used to make an impact rather than stating a truth. And then, of course, there is the trouble created when an impact statement is accepted and held to be a truth (and visa versa).

How about "Honor thy father and mother." Is this just the case? Isn't honor a bit like love, something that must be earned rather than being demanded--or expected? What if one's parents are jerks? What if they are abusive? Religious kooks? What if they are using the child as a self object? What does "honor" mean here? Treat them as they deserve? Grant them a free pass on everything? Be obedient?

Is it honoring one's parents to tell them you think they are stupid--if you do? Is it honoring them if you tell them you want to take the tuition money they have saved for you to study business and study literature instead? Or does it honor them if you are furious at them but smile politely at the dinner table?

Does it honor them if you are obedient instead of trying to figure out how to be who you are?

One lives in a working class home where all sorts of stories and myths prevail. NASCAR is revered. One gets married when one graduates from High School. Working at the gas station is reputable.

One lives in an upscale home where one's parents are business people. They acquire things and see their worth in terms of them. Money is seen as the supreme element of value. How much we enjoyed the trip is less important than how much it cost. Life is for earning, and the more the better.

One lives in a home where one's parents are artists. They are highly intelligent but poor. The house is filled with all sorts of interesting people. Those who stand in lines and have routines are not valued. Books are all over the place.

These are cartoons, but how easy is it for a child to emerge from such contexts and pursue his or her own course beyond them?

Think of the famous New Yorker cartoon entitled Map of the United States. This depicted the
five boroughs in great detail and ended at the
Hudson. Really. What else is there?

What of the common notion one should marry?
Where did that come from? This is a good idea
for everyone? For whom? We know most marriages end in divorce. Aren't we bright enough to
conceive of other options?

Homosexual marriage? Exactly how will this
destroy the foundations of society--perhaps other
than requiring an adjustment to its myths and stories?

Why is seeing differently so hard?

Consider the concept "openness to new experience." This is a factor in the Five Factor Model of
personality (FFM) (see Openness). The other factors are conscientiousness, extroversion, agree-
ableness, and neuroticism.

The openness factor seeks to make a distinction
between the creative and adventurous person as
opposed to the stable and cautions person.

Openness is a general appreciation for art, emotion, adventure, unusual ideas, imagination, curiosity, and variety of experience. The trait distinguishes imaginative people from down-to-earth, conventional people. People who are open to experience are intellectually curious, appreciative of art, and sensitive to beauty. They tend to be, compared to closed people, more creative and more aware of their feelings. They are more likely to hold unconventional beliefs. People with low scores on openness tend to have more conventional, traditional interests. They prefer the plain, straightforward, and obvious over the complex, ambiguous, and subtle. They may regard the arts and sciences with suspicion or even view these endeavors as uninteresting.

Clearly, those high in openness are more likely to embrace new things

and to be curious about what lies beyond their present experience. Those
low in openness favor security and
an acceptance of tradition. One of
the traits noticed in people high in
openness pertains to values--that is:
"the readiness to re-examine traditional social, religious, and political
values (Openness, p.2)."

In any case it is the nature of growth to reach out
and beyond the present .

There are social and political implications to this personality trait. People who are highly open to experience tend to be politically liberal
and tolerant of diversity. As a consequence, they are generally more
open to different cultures and
lifestyles. They are lower in ethno-
centrism and right wing authoritarianism (Ibid.).

The contrast between open and closed groups is increasingly apparent in recent culture. Aside from an endorsement of warring factions in order to obviate the need for critical thinking, such contrasts would seem to be the expected result of a group of people with different preferences: i.e., new or old, out versus in.

Thus, when cultures advance it would seem that open elements prevail over closed elements. If the closed elements prevailed, there would be no advancement. In this light it has long been known that new ideas and developments routinely come from the out-group instead of the in-group--where reverence for the status quo is stronger.

It may be argued, for example, the election of Barack Obama to the U.S. Presidency was the election of a more open approach to government. This election was met, again--as might be expected--by a wave of protest from more closed elements who wanted things to "go back to the way they were."

But this election signaled a cultural move toward a different stance in the world itself, a transcendence beyond at home cultural polarities. In this light, a return to self-focus and isolationism is simply not possible. The evolving nature of world cultures indicates this.

Another example is the Arab Spring uprisings where peaceful (open) demonstrations toppled closed and autocratic regimes. These uprisings caught the U.S. off guard. Why?

Clearly projecting its own tendency toward political antimony--and assuming the Arab people would be similar--U.S. policy tended to divide Arab states into 1) autocratic regimes, and 2) Muslim radicals. This view certainly seemed justified in the climate following 9/11.

But it was wrong, and the U.S. strategy of supporting autocrats because they opposed Muslim radicals simply devolved into an attempt to determine who was the worse tyrant: the ruling autocrats or the Muslim fundamentalists. In this division there was no room for the Arab people, that is the humans who are much more like we are than different.

And when the *people* rose up to demonstrate, the U.S. didn't know who they were--and had to be open and learn.

It is easy to be captured in regional, local, and cultural myths and stories, because they are all around us. They are simply assumed in what we think and do. They are endemic in American Middle Schools, where to be different is death. Such enculturation is as severe as it is pathological. Being popular is more important than breathing.

The American corporate structure frequently is autocratic and closed. "This is simply how it is done." "Power is the only realistic medium." "Don't rock the boat." "Welcome to the Navy; your job is to not make waves."

It is hard not to think something dies in the closed, something that needs to be open to live. There is something born in one's leaving where one has been. All cultures modify and evolve. Life at its core is fluid.

In fact if one is a more open sort of person who is surrounded by closed types, or visa-versa, one will likely experience oneself as being out of place. If everyone else around here is a green and I am a blue, there will be a mismatch. And this mismatch may be huge.

This is especially a problem with more closed persons, who tend to surround themselves with those who are also closed. This is so as relating to people who are the same does not require learning anything new. Open types are more comfortable with situations that are new or different.

Part of the business of psychotherapy is to discover and create alternate experiences for thoughts, feelings, attitudes, and beliefs. This is undertaken in the service of freeing people to be able to re-experience themselves in a safe but different context. The virtue of talking to an empathic and accepting person who has a different base is that it quickly illuminates one's own. What was automatic and unconscious is noticed and discussed. The world is allowed to become one of noticeable constructions.

And, of course, that is exactly what our myths and stories are: constructions. Though some are simply assumed while others are presented and defended as truths, they all have a function: either to illuminate, free, or bind.

It is the elementary myths and stories that are most able to provide illumination into our human situation. Folk or local myths and stories may either work to open us to other contexts or bind us in the present.

Since we are entering a world in which more, not less, cooperation is required between groups, remaining bound to localities and local viewpoints to the exclusion of others becomes a limitation to maximizing human potential and well-being. We are rapidly approaching the time when it is not sufficient to be a citizen of a locality. We are required to become citizens of as many localities as we can. In this way we will shift from the process of working against each other and begin to create a context in which all are (more) welcome.

REFERENCES

Campbell, J. The Inner Reaches of Outer Space: Metaphor as Myth and Religion. Harper. 1986.

Fonagy, P. An Attachment Theory Approach to Treatment of the Difficult Patient. Bull Menninger Clinic 62:147-169, 1998.

Kopping, K.P. Adolf Bastian and the Psychic Unity of Man: The Foundations of Anthropology in Nineteenth Century Germany: History and Theory of Anthropology. Vol.1. Lit Verlag. 2005.

Openness. http://en.wikipedia.org/wiki/Big_-Five_personality_traits

Russell, T. A Renegade History of the United States. Free Press, 2010.

Wittgenstein, L. Trans G.E.M. Anscombe Philosophical Investigations. Macmillan. 1953.

Zoroaster. http://en.wikipedia.org/wiki/Zoroaster

MR. CHO

> Hatred does not cease by hatred, but only by love; this is the eternal rule.
>
> --Buddha

You broke my heart, Mr. Cho.

I somehow saw it in your photograph. And then I heard it unfold in your story and the details that gradually emerged. I watched your last video. I listened to what the "experts" had to say about

121

you, and I listen to their tone as they said it. I read what you had written, and I listened to your favorite song.

The facts are clear: you were the greatest single mass-murderer in U.S. history. You erased the lives of so many beautiful people, full of promise, and dear to the point of being sacred to their families. And you made your statement, indelible as it is terrifying.

It is a statement that is almost impossibly complex.

The attack was as follows:

> The Virginia Tech massacre was a school shooting that took place on April 16, 2007, on the campus of Virginia Polytechnic Institute and State University in Blacksburg, Virginia, United States. In two separate attacks, approximately two hours apart, the perpetrator, Seung-Hui Cho, killed 32 people and wounded many others before com-

mitting suicide. The massacre is the deadliest shooting incident by a single gunman in U.S. History.

Cho used two firearms during the attacks: a 22-caliber Walther P22 semi-automatic handgun and a 9 mm semi-automatic Clock 19 handgun. The shootings occurred in separate incidents, with the first at West Ambler Johnson Hall, during which Cho killed two pupils, and the second at Norris Hall, where the other 31 deaths, including that of Cho himself, as well as all the non-lethal injuries, occurred.

Almost two hours after the first killings, Cho appeared at a nearby post office and mailed a package of writings and video recordings to NBC News; the package was postmarked 9:01 AM. He then walked to Norris Hall. In a backpack, he carried several chains, locks, a hammer, a knife, two guns, nineteen

10 and 15 round magazines, and almost 400 rounds of ammunition.

Approximately 10-12 minutes after the second attack began, Cho shot himself in the head. During this second assault, he had fired at least 174 rounds, killing 30 people and wounding 17 more. All of the victims where shot at least three times each; of the 30 killed, 28 were shot in the head. During the investigation, State Police Superintendent William Flaherty told a state panel that police found 203 live rounds in Norris Hall. 'He was well prepared to continue...," Flaherty testified (See Crime).

The reaction was profound.

The attacks received international media coverage and drew widespread criticism of U.S. laws and culture. It sparked intense debate about gun violence, gun laws,, gaps in the U.S. system for treating mental health issues, the perpetrator's state of mind, the responsibility of college administrations, privacy laws, journalism ethics, and other issues. Television news organizations that aired portions of the killer's multi-media manifesto were criticized by victims' families, Virginia law enforcement officials, and theAmerican Psychiatric Association (Ibid.).

The facts were shocking as they slowly unfolded over several days. Almost immediately interest turned toward the perpetrator. Who could have carried out such a monstrous crime, and what was the motive? Details dribbled in.

I was caught up in this story, in part, because, being a psychologist, I was immediately interested in what sort of psychological issues might lie behind these events.

Also, I had been living with a Korean woman at the time who had been abused by her native born Korean father. She was an honors university student while she lived with me. My friend, born in Los Angeles where the external culture was at tremendous odds with her home life, was routinely whipped with a rod at home for minor infractions.

She spoke often and with much feeling about the traditional Korean family culture, which, according to her, revolved around a dominant and autocratic father who demanded obedience and had final say in all matters related to the family. There was a huge emphasis placed on appearance. Thus it was important to have a family that appeared perfect, highly capable, and clearly doing well. No deviations were allowed. Duty, compliance, and work were the core elements taught.

To my ear, this sounded dysfunctional (as well as abusive).

Cho was born in Seoul, South Korea. Cho's poor but hard working family had a difficult time in the beginning.

Cho's mother was forced into an arranged marriage with his father, Sung-tae, who was 10 years older and from a very different background. She was from a well-educated family of North Korean landowners, who had been forced to flee without possessions during the Korean War; he was from a poor family in the south, but had made enough money to marry by working in Saudi Arabia for 10 years on construction sites and oil fields.

As Hyang-im was 29--a late age for a woman to find a husband in South Korea--her father told her she had to accept the proposal. "She didn't want to marry, but she gave in," said Yong-soon [Hyang-im's mother's aunt]. "Her husband was not fit for her. But she always followed and obeyed him. She never fought him, though sometimes I wish she had done." No one in the family recalls any violent behavior from

Cho or his parents that might have hinted at the carnage to come.

But they were unnerved by his sullenness..."The boy was so different from his super-intelligent older sister. His extreme shyness worried his parents..." Schoolmates interviewed by local media said they remembered Cho as quiet and nondescript. His former teacher, Noh Yong-gil, has no recollection of him (see Guardian 1).

The family decided to immigrate to the United States.

Cho Seung-Hui's family lived in a Seoul suburb in a rented basement apartment--usually the cheapest in a multi-unit building, landlord Lim Bong-ae, told Chosun Ilbo, South Korea's largest newspaper. "I didn't know what (Cho's father) did for a living. But they lived a poor life,"

Lim told the newspaper. "While em-
igrating (Cho's father) said they
were going to America because it is
difficult to live here and it's better
to live in a place where he is unknown (Chang 1997)."

Clearly the relationship between Cho's mis-
matched parents was strained. It was not a marriage of love, and perhaps not one of warmth.
Likely overshadowed by his struggling parents
and his bright sister, Cho as a child became quite
shy.

In Seoul, there was never much
money, never enough time. The
Cho family occupied a shabby two-
room basement apartment, living
frugally on the slender proceeds of a
used-book shop...In 1984, relatives
who had moved to the United States
invited the family to join them. It
took eight years to get a visa. In
1992, they arrived in Detroit and
then moved on to Centreville, Va.,

home to a bustling Korean community on the fringe of Washington.
They found jobs in the dry-cleaning
business and worked the longest of
hours...The goal, of course, was to
own one's own business. But it did
not happen for Seung-Tae Cho. He
began as a presser--an 8 a.m.-to-10
p.m. job--and that is what he is today. His wife worked in the same
capacity until a few years ago, when
she accepted a job in a high-school
cafeteria so the family could have
medical insurance...They lived in a
nondescript row house in a modest
section of town, friendly but not
overly sociable. Jeff Ahn, president
of the League of Korean-Americans
of Virginia, said the family was un-
commonly private among the throb-
bing Korean-American
community...They shunned the
more prominent Korean-language
churches, and prayed at a small
church outside of town (Kleinfield,
2007).

Such a move would be difficult for even the best-prepared and solid persons. But the Cho family found it necessary to struggle to make good in their new location.

> Cho's family worked hard to make a success of their life in the U.S. His father spent hours in the laundry, earning enough money for his children's education. His mother supplemented their income with part-time employment as a waitress at a cafeteria. Her spare time was devoted to the Korean church in Centreville, where she implored the pastor to help her son(see Guardian 1).

The struggles experienced by immigrants are legendary and this is clearly not less true in the case of Mr. Cho's parents.

In an editorial Thursday, the Hanky-oreh [Korean newspaper] said Cho's case reflected problems faced by Many South Korean immigrants in the United States.

"It is the reality of our immigrants that parents are so busy making a living that it's not easy for them to have dialogue with young children," the newspaper wrote.

"We should think about whether our society or our community abroad had been negligent in preventing conditions that could lead to such an aberration," it said (Lim, 2007).

Mr. Cho's early experiences in the United States indicate the problems he displayed early on.

Sometimes, Hyang Im Cho would become so frustrated with her son, Seung Hui Cho, that she would shake him. He rarely spoke. And when he did, it was just a few words, barely above a whisper. He never looked anyone in the eye...Life had been difficult for Cho. As an infant in South Korea, he developed whooping cough and was hospitalized with pneumonia. Doctors told the family that he had heart trouble and, when he was 3, they performed an invasive procedure to examine him. From then on Cho did not like to be touched.

In Korea, Cho had few friends he played with. But once the family moved to the United States in 1992 to provide a better education for the children, Cho became more withdrawn. If he talked to anyone at all, it was to his sister. Even then, he would never tell her what he was thinking or feeling. She knew he was being taunted for his accent and inability to speak English, as was she. But whenever she's ask him about it, would always say he was "okay."

Even that limited communication disappeared when a visitor came to the home. The family noticed that Cho's palms would become sweaty, he would freeze, would sometimes cry and was able only to nod yes or no. His parents, by then working six days a week at the dry cleaners, pressured him to talk. His mother urged him to "have more courage"...When Cho was still in elementary school, the family decided to "let him be the way he is'...(Schulte, 2007).

Rarely spoke? He avoided eye contact? Was shaken to make him speak? Was "pressured" to talk? Sweaty palms? Rarely spoke above whisper? Let him be the way he is???? Did this not seem to be a very frightened little boy?

Try as she might--with countless visits to counselors and psychologists, treatment with antidepressants or art therapy, and attempts to find

134

him friends at basketball camp or tai
Kwan do or church—no one could
break through.

Like any mother, she wanted her
son to fit in. Like any immigrant,
she felt that no sacrifice was too
great to make sure he found a place
for himself in this new country,
even if it meant overcoming the
deeply ingrained stigma in Korean
culture of admitting mental illness
(Ibid.)

Generalizations aside, it is still difficult to imagine no one sensed the terrible isolation in this boy.
despite the fact it might be labeled a "mental illness." What about the attachment pattern here?

In 1997, the summer before he entered middle school and on the
school's recommendation, the family took Cho to the Center for Mul-
ticultural Human Services, where
he saw an art therapist and a psy-

chiatrist who diagnosed a severe social anxiety disorder. "It was painful to see," one of the psychiatrists told the panel. The Chos took turns leaving work early to get their son to his sessions every week. In art therapy, Cho made houses out of clay that had no windows or doors. Sometimes, when the therapist explained that his artwork showed how inadequate he must feel, *Cho's eyes would fill with tears.*

In, 1999, during the spring of the eighth grade, the clay houses morphed into disturbing caves and tunnels. Cho wrote in a school assignment about wanting to "repeat Columbine." A psychiatrist diagnosed selective mutism--the inability to speak in certain circumstances because of profound social anxiety—and prescribed Paroxetine, an anti-depressant. *The drug treatment was discontinued after one year because Cho seemed much better* (Ibid) [my italics].

So Mr. Cho *did* respond. He responded to empathic interpretation and also to antidepressant medication.

There are further facts involved:

> Students who knew him as far back as middle school remember a dramatically uncommunicative boy who never spoke, not even to teachers. Some remember class-mates derisively offering dollar bills to Cho if he would just talk. The band director would urge him to play his trombone more loudly and to hold his head up.

> "Teachers would call on him, and he wouldn't respond," recalled Sam Linton, 21, a freshman at New River Community College near Virginia Tech, who attended classes and

shared a homeroom with Cho at Stone Middle School in Centreville. "He would just sit there until they would call on somebody else."

James Duffy, 21, a Virginia Tech junior who also attended Stone, said the first time he ever heard Cho speak was on television Wednesday night, when NBC aired the recordings he had mailed in the middle of the rampage. "That was also the firsttime I ever saw an expression on his face," Duffy recalled.

Other students recalled that he carried violent writings in his notebooks. He wore "geeky" clothes, not stylish or popular, the kind his parents might have picked out, Linton recalled...

David Gearhart, 21, a junior at Virginia Tech who attended Stone Middle with Cho, said Cho's antisocial [asocial?] behavior prompted teasing from other kids.

"We might have cracked a couple of jokes, nothing to his face for sure. Nothing very serious.   We would just say, 'Did you see Seung say nothing again today?'   Something like that."

Gearhart remembers a friend seeing a paper fall out of Cho's notebook. "It had all kinds of hate writing," he said (Ibid.).

In the face of such overwhelming evidence of pain and anguish, nothing happened.   Mr. Cho went on to High School.

Yet there is one account that is different.

Mr. Kim, a 23-year old senior at Kyung Hee University in Seoul, told the Joong Ang Daily that Cho was an athletic student who excelled at mathematics and English.

He was even held up as a role model by his teachers, said Mr. Kim, who was friends with him for three years when they attended the Poplar Tree Elementary School in Fairfax County, Virginia.

'Teachers said Seung-hui finished the three-year program in a year and a half, and they used him as an exemplary model for other students'... (see Anon 1).

During this time Cho's father rarely said anything about his family. He never took more than a day off at a time. "He was working too hard, just working, working," [one of Cho's father's bosses] said. But at lunch breaks, he would frequently boast of his daughter. "He was very proud of her. He always talked about her," she said (Ibid.).

What about the other child, the "ghost?"

As for Cho's sister, Sun Kyung, classmates of hers at Princeton could not remember her ever talking about her family. One friend said he was "surprised to learn she had a brother, as she rarely, if ever mentioned her family (Ibid.)

High school did not help Seung-Hui Cho surmount his miseries. He went to Westfield HighSchool, one of the largest schools in Fairfax County. He was scrawny and looked younger than his age. He was unresponsive in class, and unwilling to speak.

And that haunted face.

Classmates recall some teasing and bullying over his taciturn nature. The few times he was required to speak for a class assignment, students mocked his poor English and deep-throated voice.

And so he chose invisibility. Neighbors would spot him shooing baskets by himself. When they said hello, he ignored them, as if he were not there. "[It was] Like he had a broken heart," said Abdul Shash, a next-door neighbor (Kleinfield, 2007).

It is little surprise a young man who is utterly different, who has a speech and language problem, who is afraid of others because of how they treat him, a young man with little self esteem or positive affective coloring of the self representation, who likely suffers from an avoidant attachment, who has no empathic confidant, and is routinely bullied for sport, would be angry.

In high school, Cho Seung-Hui almost never opened his mouth. When he finally did, his class-mates laughed, pointed at him and said: "Go back to China."

Classmates in Virginia, whereCho grew up, said he was teased and picked on, apparently because of shyness and his strange, mumbly way of speaking.

142

Once, in English class at Wesfield High School in Chantilly, Va., when the teacher had the students read aloud, Cho looked down when it was his turn, said Chris Davids, a Virginia Tech senior and high school classmate. After the teacher threatened him with an F or participation, Cho began reading in a strange, deep voice that sounded "like he had something in his mouth," Davids said.

"The whole class started laughing and pointing and saying, 'Go back to China,'" Davids said.

There were just some people who were really mean to him and they would push him down and laugh at him," Roberts said. "He didn't speak English really well and they would really make fun of him (Apuzzo and Cohen, 2007)."

Mr. Cho, of course, was enduring this without any meaningful support or connection. Nonetheless, My Cho graduated from a demanding honors program and entered Virginia Tech University.

His fortunes did not improve at college.

> When Mr. Cho entered Virginia Tech, which is crouched in the Blue Ridge Mountains of south-west Virginia, his parents drove him to school with guarded expectations. Perhaps he would no longer retreat to video games and playing basketball alone the way he did at home. Perhaps college might crack the mystery of who he was, extract him from his suffocating cocoon and make him talk (Kleinfield, 2007).

It did not. Mr. Cho continued his odd behavior as well as admitting some new ones. He continued his essentially mute existence.

In his freshman year at Virginia Polytechnic Institute and State University (Virginia Tech), Cho enrolled as an undergraduate major in business information technology, a program that included "a combination of computer science and management coursework offered by the Pamplin College of Business." The program was listed as No. 6 on the "list of majors with the highest median starting salary after graduation." By his senior year, Cho was majoring in English. Virginia Tech declined to divulge details about Cho's academic record and why he changed his major, citing privacy laws.

Fellow students described Cho as a "quiet" person who "would not respond if someone greeted him." Student Julie Poole recalled the first day of a literature class the previous year when the students introduced themselves one by one. When it was

Cho's turn to introduce himself, he did not speak. According to Poole, the professor looked at the sign-in sheet and found that, whereas everyone else had written out their names, Cho had written only a question mark. Poole added that "we just really knew him as the question mark kid" (see Cho 1).

After Mr. Cho's massacre and death, his sister provided an important piece of the puzzle.

Cho began his college career as a business information technology major but, by the time he was a sophomore, decided to switch to English, which was one of his weakest subjects.   Nevertheless, he was convinced that he could be a great writer. He had written a novel, which he described to teachers as "sort of like Tom Sawyer except that it's really silly and pathetic," the report said.

146

Later that year, after his sister
found a rejection letter from a New
York publishing house, she noticed
that he became increasingly depressed and detached. His English
grades ranged from B's to D's, and
his rage grew as he felt no one understood him or his talent (Schulte,
2007).

And, again, there was no one to help or encourage, to help him learn rejection letters are routine,
even for successful writers. And also there was no
one to help him continue his clear need to succeed
and make an important mark.

Further insights can be obtained through the
following remarks of Mr. Cho's roommates.

The sunglasses. The buzz haircut
she gave himself in his room. The
calls to his roommates in which he
pretended he was somebody named

"Question Mark," and they all knew it was Seung.

Andy Koch was fed up with his roommate, Seung Hui Cho, he recalled yesterday in a telephone interview from Blacksburg. "Who does this?" Koch said to himself.

Amid the social whirl and the all-nighters and the classes, Cho first began to strike people as not quite right. Koch, 21, has emerged as among the first to alert school authorities about Cho. Since Cho's rampage, he has replayed the events of 2005 over and over, wondering if he might have done more..

Koch said Cho was dropped off at the start of school with little family fanfare. "Just a shy and quiet kid," he said (Ruane, 2007).

Koch stated the following memories.

Koch remembers taking Cho out to some parties at the start of the fall semester in 2005. He introduced Cho to friends, but the sullen roommate didn't say much. At one party, Cho did get tipsy enough that he opened up and began talking about his virtual love life.

He said he had an imaginary girlfriend named Jelly, and that she was "a supermodel that lived in space." Jelly had a nickname for Cho-- Spanky.

Once, Koch knocked on Cho's door looking for his roommate, John. The door was locked, and Seung wouldn't open it up.

"I'm in here with my girlfriend and we're making out," he said.

"Who says that kind of stuff?" the junior from Richmond asked.

Then there was the beer-pong game. It was down to the final shot, and it was Cho's turn to sink a ping-pong ball in a beer-filled cup from across a table. Cho stared down a cup of beer and nailed the shot with amazing accuracy.

"Usually there's a lot of smack talk going on and he didn't even blink an eye," Koch said.

The incident offered a glimpse of the calm Cho's victims witnessed as he marched from desk to desk, room to room, firing his two guns into his defenseless targets.

A couple of months later during Thanksgiving break, Koch's phone rang. It was Cho.

"I didn't know why he called, and I was like 'What's up?' He goes, 'I'm vacationing with Vladimir Putin. I was like, 'Really? I think he lives in Russia.' He's like, 'Yeah, we're in

North Carolina.' I'm like, 'I'm pretty sure that's not possible Seung.'"

And that was a relatively innocent conversation compared with some of Koch's other experiences.

One night, he was awakened by police officers banging on the door.

Cho had been harassing a female student over the Internet and was talking about suicide, and the police showed up to intervene. When Cho did the same to a friend of Koch's, and the woman contacted the police, Cho sent a text message to his suitemate.

"I might as well kill myself," he wrote. Koch called the police again, and Cho was committed for what turned out to be a too--short psychological evaluation (Breed and Kahn, 2007)

After the shooting another report was made by Mr. Grewal who also lived with Cho.

> The basic story was this: Cho was a loner who rarely said a word, and when he did speak, it was one-word conversations. He sometimes watched game shows and Spike TV, usually by himself. He had been getting up earlier than normal lately, by 5 a.m. in the days prior to the shooting. He apparently started lifting weights in February.

> But a mass murderer?

> "He didn't seem like a guy who could even hold up two guns and shoot really. He was not athletic in any way," Grewal said (Ibid.).

Mr Cho also had troubles in his classes. Aside from his overall silence, he stayed to himself all the time. His writing could be disturbing.

Lucinda Roy said that in October of 2005 she was contacted as head of the English Department by a p r o-fessor [Giovanni] who was disturbed by a piece of his [Cho's] writing. Ms. Roy, rebuffed by Mr. Cho, contacted the campus police, counseling services, student affairs and officials in her department. Ms. Roy described the writing as a "veiled threat rather than something explicit."

University officials told her she could drop Mr. Cho from the class. Or, they said, she could tutor him individually, and she agreed to do so three times from October to December 2005. During those sessions, she said in an interview, he always wore sunglasses and a baseball cap pulled low.

"He seemed to be crying behind his sunglasses," she said (Fenandez and Santora, 2007).

Amazingly during these sessions, Roy was able to get Mr. Cho to open up about his feelings of isolation.

"You seem so lonely," she told him once. "Do you have any friends?"

"I am lonely," he replied. "I don't have any friends (Breed, 2007)."

Mr. Cho's difficulties with Nikki Giovanni, a gifted poet who taught at the university, were substantial. She said other students had left her class due to Mr. Cho.

In Giovanni's class, the students, including Cho, recited poems they had written. Days later, only seven of 70 or so students showed up for class. She asked why the others didn't come and was told that they were afraid of Cho (Horwitz, 2007).

Concerned, she wrote to Ms Roy.

"I was willing to resign before I was going to continue with him, Ms. Giovanni said in an interview with CNN. "People just quit coming to class, a couple of students absolutely quit coming to class.:"

Ms. Roy told CNN that she "felt strongly that he was suicidal." She said: It was really like talking to a hole sometimes, as though the person wasn't really there." Ms. Giovanni said Mr. Cho did not scare her ["I was not afraid of this child."], but she once instructed him to stop his disturbing writings. "He said 'You can't make me,' and I said 'Yeah, I can (Ibid.).'"

Seeking to practice his skills as a writer, Mr. Cho wrote two disturbing plays in another class.

The following quotes are from Cho's play Richard McBeef.

RICHARD

What is it you want from me, what do you want me to do? Why are you so angry at me--

JOHN

Why am I so angry at you? Because you murdered my father so you can get into my mom's pants!--

RICHARD

Now hold on right there mister. It was a boating accident. I did everything I could to try to save your father.

JOHN

Bullshit! Are you always full of shit, McBeef? I can see that you are by the extra fat you have packed on! You MURDERED my father and covered it up! You committed a conspiracy. Just like what the government has done to John Lennon and Marilyn Monroe.

Also:

JOHN

(In his room, he smiles and throws darts on the target that is the face of Richard.)

I hate him. Must kill Dick. Must kill Dick. Dick must die. Kill Dick. Richard McBeef. What kind of name is that? What an asshole name. I don't like it. And look at his face. What an asshole face. I don't like his face at all. You don't think I can kill you, Dick? You don't think I can kill you? Gotcha. Got the one eye-- Got the other eye.

Additionally, consider the following from another play: Mr. Brownstone.

JANE

There is like no safe place for us to hang out. We can't hang out in front of the grocery store, we can't hang out at the park, we can't hang out in the street. The only place where we are safe from that him is behind the shitty dumpster.

JOHN

Mr. Brownstone.

JOE

That old fart just won't leave us alone.

JANE

He has to make our lives miserable.

JOHN

I'd like to kill him.

JANE

I'll be damn if he doesn't die. I wish
that old fart would have a heart attack and drop dead like old people
are supposed to.

JOHN

Make room for the new generation,
you old fart!

And:

MR. BROWNSTONE
(Lowering his voice.)

You fucking little kids. Don't you
publicly humiliate me! You know

159

what I can do to you at school on
Monday?

JOHN

I feel a satanic presence around me.
Do you guys feel it?

JOE

Absolutely.

Of course it is difficult to know just what is creative writing and what is genuine threat. Imagination is one thing; action is another.

In interviews with six members of
the English faculty who had Mr.
Cho in a class or had been in close
contact with him, they described
how as early as September 2005 and
as recently as September 2006, they
found themselves struggling to define the line between a legitimate
work of self-expression and one of

violent or sick imagery that needed to be restrained (Santora and Hauser, 2007).

Not only did Mr. Cho manage to be a problem in his classes, he also had difficulty in his interactions with women.

He became fixated on several real female students [in addition to Jelly]. Two of them complained to the police that he was calling them, showing up at rooms and bombarding them with instant messages. They found him bother-some but not threatening. After the second complaint against him in December 2005, the police came by and told him to stop (Kleinfield, 2007).

On one occasion, however, Cho's messages unnerved a woman in his class.

She said [to Police] Mr. Cho knew things about her family that would be difficult to know without serious effort. For instance, he knew what sports her siblings played in high school (Santora and Hauser, 2007).

Following this run-in with the police as well as his suicidal statement to his roommate, Mr. Cho was sent to an off-campus mental health center. There he met with a counselor who recommended involuntary commitment. A judge then signed an order deeming Mr. Cho a danger [suicide], and he was sent to Carilon St. Albans Psychiatric Hospital in Radford, Virginia for an evaluation.

Mr Cho was evaluated by a psychiatrist at this facility. He apparently deemed Mr. Cho "mentally ill but not an imminent threat." As a result a judge referred Mr. Cho for outpatient treatment instead of commitment (Kleinfield, 2007). This would have been routine.

Back in his dorm room, Mr. Cho played his favorite song over and over.

SHINE

Give me a word
Give me a sign
Show me where to look
Tell what will I find (will I find)

Lay me on the ground
Fly me in the sky
Show me where to look
Tell me what will I find (will I find)

Oh, heaven let your light shine down
(x4)

Love is in the water
Love is in the air
Show me where to go
Tell me will love be there (love be
there)

Teach me how to speak
Teach me how to share
Teach me where to go
Tell me will love be there (love be

there)

Oh, heaven let your light shine down
(x4)

I'm going to let it shine (x2)
Heaven's little light gonna shine on
me
Yea yea heaven's little light gonna
shine on me
Its gonna shine, shine on me
Its gonna shine, come on in shine
(Roland)

School was drawing to an end for Mr. Cho. He had dreamed of becoming a famous writer in order to make his mark on the world. His efforts had not yielded the acclaim he desired. What would he do? A famous writer would make his parents proud, equal the achievements of his sister, and go some distance to assuage the hurt he felt at the hands of his peers.

If he left school, he would be turned loose into the "larger" hostile world where he had no reason to think anything would be measurably different for him. Others succeeded. He did not. As he looked out, he saw nothing.

Mr. Cho bought a gun. He bought another. He rented a van for a month. He bought numerous rounds of ammunition.

> Over the next few weeks, he fulfilled the rest of his shopping list. Investigators said he went to the Wal-Mart in Christianburg on March 31, April 7, April 8, and April 13. During those visits, he bought cargo pants, sunglasses and .22 caliber ammunition. He also bought a hunting knife, gloves, a phone item and a granola bar. He visited Dick's Sporting Good for extra magazines of ammunition. He got chains at Home Depot (Ibid.)."

In all, Mr. Cho spent several thousand dollars in preparation for his massacre, most of it charged to a credit card. He checked into two different inns in two days.   In the latter, he made photographs and a video.   He assembled these along with a "manifesto" which he later mailed to NBC news.

> He assembled a package, and in it
> were QuickTime videos of himself
> 43 photographs and an 1,800 word
> statement outlining his place in a
> world he saw arrayed against him.
> Many of the snapshots were of him
> brandishing guns--at nothing, at the
> camera, at himself.   One showed
> him with a hammer.   There was a
> photo of bullets standing lined up as
> if soldiers awaiting inspection (Kle-
> infield, 2007).

Wearing his gear and brandishing his pistols Mr. Cho finally uttered his pain.

> "You have vandalized my heart,
> raped my soul and torched my con-
> science," he said into the camera,
> looking down occasionally to read

from his manifesto. "You thought it was one pathetic boy's life you were extinguishing. Thanks to you, I die like Jesus Christ, to inspire generations of the weak and the defenseless people."

"I didn't have to do this. I could have left. I could have fled," he said. "But no, I will no longer run.:

"It's not for me. For my children, for my brothers and sisters...I did it for them."

"You had a hundred billion chances and ways to have avoided today," he said. "But you decided to spill my blood. You forced me into a corner and gave me only one option. The decision was yours. Now you have blood on your hands that will never wash off.:"

"Your Mercedes wasn't enough, you brats," he said. "Your golden necklaces weren't enough you snobs.   Your trust funds wasn't enough. Your vodka and cognac wasn't enough. All your debaucheries weren't enough. Those weren't enough to fulfill your hedonistic needs. You had everything (O'Neill, 2007).

Also:

"Do you know what it feels like to be spit on your face and have trash shoved down your throat? Do you know what it feels like to dig your own grave? Do you know what it feels like to have your throat slashed from ear to ear? Do you know what it feels like to be torched alive? Do you know what it's like to be humiliated and be impaled upon a cross and left to bleed to death for your amusement (Anon 2)?

The shootings occurred in two parts. The first occurred at West Ambler Johnson Hall, a student dorm. The second occurred at Norris Hall, a classroom located across the campus from the dormitory.

Sometime around 9:30, Mr. Cho stepped inside Norris Hall. He was wearing cargo pants, a sweatshirt, an ammunition vest and a maroon cap, the school color. He carried a backpack--a receipt for one of the guns stuffed inside--and he was carrying chains and some knives. On one arm was inscribed Ax Ishmael, a name whose significance has not been determined but might be a Biblical allusion.

He unfurled the chains and wrapped them around the interior handles of the doors. The entrance secured, he mounted the stairs to the second floor and the classrooms. Second period had begun.

The stairs he took emptied into the short end of the L, where there were seven class rooms. Two were vacant, and five were in session. Rooms 204, 205, 206, 207, 211. Gun drawn, he forged into four of them. Inside of 10 to 15 minutes, forensics evidence concluded, he fired more than 175 rounds in killing 30 people, the worst slaughter of its kind in the history of the country (Kleinfield, 2007).

Mr. Cho had made his statement.

Press reports held either than Mr. Cho was a madman or that he was a "typical serial killer," both dismissive. The genuine tragedy of the loss of so many vibrant, loved, and gifted people was all but overwhelming. Students gathered. Vigils were held. Commissions were impaneled to look into the affair.

And Mr. Cho's statement to his parents also hit its mark. Immediately after the event.

170

"He has made the world weep. We are living a nightmare," said a statement issued by Cho's sister, Sun-Kyung Cho, on the family's behalf.

"We are humbled by this darkness. We feel hopeless, helpless and lost. This is someone that I grew up with and loved. Now I feel like I didn't know this person," Cho's sister said. "We have always been a close, peaceful and loving family. My brother was quiet and reserved, yet struggled to fit in. We never could have envisioned that he was capable of so much violence (Anon 3).

They too, as countless other parents of students at Virginia Tech, had spent the day trying to reach Mr. Cho in his cell-phone, but in vain.

The Chos' fears were confirmed when police officers, FBI agents, and a chaplain showed up that night at their Centreville town-house.

But the news was worse than they had imagined (Somashekhar and Horwitz, 2007).

The family went into hiding after the incident. They did give a statement to the panel created by Governor Timothy M. Kaine to investigate the tragedy.

In the emotional three-hour interview, Hyang Im described her struggle to socialize Seung Hui, who rarely spoke as a child in South Korea and withdrew even more after the family came to the United States when he was 8.

Hyang Im, with her daughter translating, told Sood [Aradhana A. "Bela" Sood, medical director of a children's treatment center at Virginia Commonwealth University] how she had tried unsuccessfully to find friends for her son. She later turned to psychiatry, despite the stigma--in Korean and American cultures--of mental illness. She and her husband worried when Seung Hui decided, against the advice of a counselor, to go away to Blacksburg.

The parents told Sood about their shock when they learned, after his death, of his violent writings: the red flags raised by professors and students who said they were afraid of him; and his brief hospitalization after a judge determined he was a suicide risk.

Had they known, "we would have taken him home and made him miss a semester to get this looked at," the Chos told Sood. "But we just did not know...about anything being wrong (Ibid.)

PART II

What is to be made of this? Mr. Cho's story is involved and heart-wrenching on so many levels. Barring any evidence of organic abnormality, which seems unlikely, what is it that led to this boy experiencing so much fear and anger?

There are clues. It would seem his parents had a strained relationship. It is likely neither were happy in their marriage, especially the mother. If so, the cultural expectations in which she lived would have urged her to keep this well hidden--despite the psychological consequences that would have entailed (i.e., "double messages"). The Cho's had a daughter, who by any measure was clearly superior. The cultural view of such a child would also be extremely positive.

The parents were very poor and were no doubt beset by the stresses and worries such a situation entails. The second child was wanted? Unwanted? At any rate the very young Mr. Cho did not

174

seem to "take hold." This was not so much a "failure to thrive" syndrome, as Mr. Cho seemed physically healthy. It appears, on the other hand, he did not attach emotionally to his mother.

Though he was beautiful and well behaved, there does not seem to have been any warmth in his life. According to Bowlby (1988) and Fonagy (2001), children need an empathic warmth from their care-taker in order to feel safe. Such empathic warmth teaches the child the world can be an okay place where one might enter and play. Absence of such an "attachment" leaves the child with an experi-ence of a cold world where one is not at all sure it is safe to enter and play.

Attachment experts speak of the importance of how the child is "held in the mind" of the parent. Is the child a wondrous being? Is the child an un-wanted pain? Is the child a delight? A burden? A replacement for a husband? This is thought to be critical as the first sense of self one develops is the self one can find in the parent.

Clearly taking delight in an empathically emo-tional connection of self to self with the child is an entirely different thing from an outside to outside (i.e., "thing") connection--if "connection" is even appropriate here. That is, one is either a delightful person or is another object, such as a lamp.

Further, experiencing an empathic, resonant warmth as an infant is an essential ingredient in the formation of good self esteem. One internalizes how wonderful others think one is. Conversely in a cold and empathy-less environment, one internalizes an empty sense of esteem.

The Korean culture highly stresses appearance and conformity. This is not a stress on *persons*. It is not unreasonable Mr. Cho's parents stressed the same. His behavior, different from the norm, likely would have caused concern on this count alone. Further, there is a cultural stigma against "mental illness," whatever that is--or is assumed to be. Whatever it may be, it is clearly a bad thing. It is not something like "excess worry" or "fear, shyness, and hesitation and a world I have never been taught is safe."

This would have made Mr. Cho a "problem." It is not impossible to imagine he was thought of more as a problem than he was thought of as a person.

Further, it is rare for *persons*, with their humanity, to be considered in an authoritarian, top down, structure. As Benjamin (1988) has argued: any deviation from an emotionally empathic resonance ("recognition") involves domination. Here, if I dominate you, I erase you; if I comply with your bid for domination, I erase me.

The appearance of order is achievable this way, but only at the horrendous cost of leaving no place for the human.

In a dysfunctional family, which runs on these rules, the emphasis is on appearance, not on reality. One struggles to be a "good kid" instead of the "real kid" one is. The good kid, after all, is *never* the real kid (nor is the "bad kid").

Mr. Cho does not seem to have "taken hold" of the interpersonal situation enough, to indulge in any of these behaviors. There was a part of him that just wasn't playing.

Such a development would have relegated him to a position essentially *outside* the mainstream. It is as if he was *afraid* of the mainstream from the start. It is as if he needed someone to genuinely and empathically *find him* and help him learn there *could* be safe experiences with others--and how to do them.

His problem was interpersonal. He was smart. He was capable. He was not mean (at least early on). But no reach was adequate. It was as if he was just supposed to fit all by himself. No training necessary.

Throughout Mr. Cho's childhood his father worked long hours, and therefore was not available to provide the functions of connection, help, and warmth a father can provide. His mother's role is less clear. The amount of work the parents performed increased dramatically in the United States. Mr. Cho, we may assume, was frequently left with himself.

There is, in fact, a "Father's School" for Korean fathers that teaches them how to become more "emotionally aware."

"Traditionally, in the Korean family, the father is very authoritarian,"

Joon Cho, a program volunteer, told me a few weeks before this session of Father School began. "They're not emotionally linked with their children or their wife. They're either workaholics, or they're busy enjoying their own hobbies or social activities. Family always comes last (Laporte, 2011, see also in a similar light: Chua, 2011)."

Mr. Cho's parents seemed to have held some belief in magical solutions. For example, the move to the U.S. would make things better. Going to college would solve the dilemma at last.

Mr. Cho's mother *pressured* him to speak. She *shook* him. Scarcely are these empathic forms of interaction or connection. .

Further, Mr. Cho endured an invasive procedure as a young child in a hospital. Subsequently, he would not allow anyone to touch him. Such traumatic events routinely have far reaching consequences even for someone who has some sense there can be safety around other people. For someone like Mr. Cho, who was basically already alone, it would have been overpowering.

Nor were the psychological aspects of this trauma treated. The feelings of being a helpless victim routinely lead to omnipotent fantasies and desires to become the strong one in the face of helpless others (identification with the aggressor).

At age eight he was taken from his familiar surroundings and plunged into an alien culture. This was a culture, furthermore, in which he was mocked and ridiculed for being different. Again, with no one he could trust to turn to for empathic support, he simply did what he had to do: survive.

He relied on himself, since he could rely on no one else. How his teachers dealt with his being mocked and ridiculed is not clear. Obviously it did significant damage. This would be especially true for one whose sense of self worth was not high in the first place. Not having internalized a sense of worth that would serve him in most situations, Mr. Cho would have been left to seek this sense of worth from others. When he received scorn and ridicule from others instead, his sense of worth would have suffered tremendously.

In short Mr. Cho had no safe harbor anywhere, unless he kept to himself and tried to soothe himself as best he could.

In Middle School he finally received some professional help--and it worked. This is a tremendously important fact. He cried in response to an empathic interpretation about how difficult his life must be. He also apparently showed "improvement" secondary to a run of anti-depressant medication.

This response to empathic treatment suggests a way Mr. Cho cold have been helped in a major way. It also suggests the lack of such treatment elsewhere in his life. But this time it *happened*! Contact was made. The interaction was safe enough Mr. Cho allowed his soul to be seen. One can only imagine the outcome had this treatment been allowed to continue. Over a consistent period of time, Mr. Cho could have learned the world *can* be different. Other people *can* be different. They *can* get it. They *can* be warm. But it was stopped. Why?

Goulston suggested the importance of genuine empathic listening:

As a psychiatrist for 25 years, I have observed that people just weren't listening. I have noticed that people have a deep need to be listened to and cared for, but often don't want to develop the ability to listen and care for others.

I've seen people negotiating more than relating. Relating requires pausing and listening to what someone else is saying without any other agenda other than under-standing exactly what they meant to say. The listening you do vali-dates that what they meant to say is worthy of being listened to. Being actually listened to instead of just heard is very healing to the human spirit.

Continuing to listen deeply is the only thing that keeps aloneness and

182

loneliness away. As soon as you stop listening and stop caring, aloneness and loneliness come back, and alienation is right behind it (Fitzgerald, 2009).

Meanwhile in middle school and also in high school, the soul-crushing demeaning continued at a steady pace. Mr. Cho couldn't fight back. He had no one he could trust to talk about these things. The rage just built up inside as he tried to find ways to endure what was not a safe environment at all.

It is typical for people who have an adequate sense of self to feel they are okay--just as they are. It is also typical for those who do not feel adequate just as they are to feel they have to *do something* in order to be okay (contingent self esteem). Mr. Cho, sadly, fell into the second category. He couldn't just be there; he had to be vacationing with Vladimir Putin. He couldn't be a contributing person; he had to be a great writer, &c.

And, in terms of his culture, he had to do something that mattered. It couldn't be ordinary. It is not surprising that when he found he couldn't be a great writer, he had to find something else at which he could be great. Nothing small or ordinary would do.

By the time Mr. Cho was in college it is likely he had virtually no experiences of himself being of worth to fall back on. He was worse than a nobody. He was an *unwelcome* nobody. And he had begun to believe this was his identity. Instead of seeking an exit from his situation, he *lived* it. He became the question mark. It is not unreasonable he took himself to be the weirdo others took him to be.

Mr. Cho's story illustrates so clearly why early intervention is important. The empathy he so desperately sought, he would have distrusted. Typical of children who have been traumatized, it would be difficult to establish trust with him. But the opening finally occurred in middle school. As this was ignored and his negative experiences continued, treatment would have become even more difficult.

Mr. Cho appears to have developed essentially two parts of himself. One might be called the

184

"coping self" which was the part that was in contact with the daily world and dealt with it in his own idiosyncratic fashion. The other was more primitive and might be called the "real self." This consisted of the frightened little kid who was enraged at the world and others who would not find a place for him--who had never thought to find a place for him.

While the coping self would have been allowed to attend school and deal with the context, the real self would have been arrested at the beginning when it became frightened and backed away from interpersonal regions. Almost certainly this real self would feel abandoned and hurt. Repeated woundings would have engendered an ever-growing rage at the insult the real self was feeling. For such a person with an extreme history like Mr. Cho's, this rage would be enough to create disaster.

It is this primitive part that somehow must be contacted and treated with empathic resonance and welcome. Containing such rage is no simple task.

It did not happen.

Certainly not all parents are equipped to make such connections. For some, even tender feelings are troublesome. When physical survival is paramount, it is easy to neglect psychological factors. And we grow. As adults we are surrounded by those with varying degrees of psychological issues. We try to take them in stride. The range of parents insures this range of experiences. No one gets a choice in this. We do what we can with what we've got.

How many children experience adequate empathic resonance and connection with their parents? How many of us are heard? Really heard, beyond superficial acquaintance? How many of us have a part of ourselves we are afraid to share?

Still given the obvious pain with which Mr. Cho lived, it is astounding vigorous efforts toward a solution were not undertaken. But who would have done this? Who, in Mr. Cho's context could have had the awareness or capacity to make this happen?

Mr. Cho's case is a comment on our culture. We simply do not do well with this sort of issue. *We* are the mockers instead of the helpers. At the same time, we feel *we* are not responsible for such disaster; it is only some nut-case. Mr. Cho's roommates and acquaintances asked if they could have done more. The answer is yes. We could all do more.

Camus (1992) argued that in order for a society to legitimately execute someone, the society has to be innocent of the crimes that person commits. But this, as he knew, is ultimately not true of any society. In some important sense the guilt belongs to everyone. And so it is with Mr. Cho. And so it is with each of us.

REFERENCES

Anon 1. "Classmates laughed at him when he spoke." 04-22-2007.

Anon 2. "'You Forced Me Into a Corner," Cho Says." Washington Post. 04-19-2007.

Anon 3. "Gunman's Family Says It Feels 'Hopeless" and "Lost.'" New York Times, 04-20-2007.

Apuzzo, M., and Cohen, S. "Experts call bullied Cbo a textbook case." Salt Lake Tribune. 04-20-2077.

Benjamin,J. The Bonds of Love: Psychoanalysis, Feminism, and the Problem of Domination. Pantheon. 1988.

Bowlby, J. A Secure Base: Parent-Child Attachment and Healthy Human Development. Basic. 1988.

Breed, A.G. "Professor Had Expelled Gunman From Class." Washington Post. 04-18-2007.

Breed, A.G. and Kahn, C. "Those Closest to Cho Return to School." Associated Press. 04-22-2007.

Camus, A. The Rebel: An Essay on Man in Revolt. Vintage, 1992.
g, J-S. "Gunman's Family Had Hard Life in Korea." Washington Post. 04-18-1997.

Cho !. http://en.wikipedia.org/wiki/Seung-Hui_-Cho

Chua, A. Battle Hymn of the Tiger Mother. Penguin. 2011.

Fernandez, M. and Santora, M. "Gunman Showed Signs of Anger." New York Times. 04-18-2007.

Fitzgerald, P. "A Psychiatrist, Executive Coach And FBI Hostage Negotiation Trainer Provides The Secret To Getting Through To Anyone." Huffington Post. 09-09-2009.

Fonagy, P. Attachment Theory and Psychoanalysis. Other. 2001.

Guardian 1. "Family of Virginia Tech Killer Cho
Seung-hui Were Concerned About His Brooding
As a Boy." Guardian Unlimited. 04-19-2007.

Horwitz, S. "Paper by Cho Exhibits Disturbing
Parallels to Shootings, Sources Say." Washington
Post. 04-29-2007.

Kleinfield, N.R. "Before Deadly Rage, a Life
Consumed by a Troubling Silence. New York
Times. 04-22-2007.

Laporte, N. "The Korean Dads' 12-Step
Program." New York Times. 05-06-2011.

Lim, B-M. "Virginia Shooter Spoke Little As
Child." Washington Post. 04-22-2007.

O'Neill, H. "Cho Offers Glimpse Into Tortured
Soul." Washington Post. 04-18-2007

Roland, E. Shine. Sugarfuzz Music.

Santora, M. and Hauser, C. "Anger of KIller Was on Exhibit in His Writings." New York Times. 04-20-2007.

Schulte, B. "Killer's Parents Describe Attempts Over the Years to Help Isolated Son."Washington Post. 08-31-2007.

Somashekhar, S. and Horwitz, "A Year After Massacre, Family Lives 'in Darkness.'" Washington Post. 04-12-2008.

THE TWO SECTORS AND THE PROBLEM OF POWER

"Let us, on both sides, lay aside all arrogance.   Let us not, on either side, claim that we have already discovered the truth."

--St. Augustine

THE TWO SECTORS

Past contexts and experiences can be internalized and remain effectively operative in one's behavior long after the original context or experience has changed. These internalized contexts operate in an unconscious way and thus avoid detection.

The distinction I am looking for separates two kinds of thought processes and hence two different ontologies and experiences of the world. The two groups I want to consider are: 1) a life primarily centered around an inclusive search for what is new and different as opposed to 2) a life centered around opposing the above group and attempting to keep things the same (valorizing tradition).

Thus one group attempts to widen perspectives and seek inclusion of as many views as possible as compared to a group that seeks to protect itself against these others. It is a difference, if you will, between the "many" and the "one against the many."

There is a mismatch between these two positions in the following way. As a rule, keep things the same us versus them position only has the perspective of an us versus them world. This is the case as everything that isn't *us* is therefore considered *them*. Journeys beyond the self sector are coded as experiences of "them" instead of being accrued as parts of an expanding experience of self. The self, in fact, does not seek to expand. The diversity position, on the other hand, has had experience of more than one context, has found worth in these, and is therefore interested in including new and different groups in the experiential field. The inclusive group actually and automatically prefers the diversity position to the us-them position. The inclusive position is interested in including the us-them position as one option-- but it cannot be the *only* (approved) option as required by the us-them people.

Many conflicts occur when these positions are thrown together. A diversity child may be raised in a us-them context, school system, or culture (as was the case in my own past). Or an us-them child may be in a diversity requiring school or profession.

Further, the us-them position is more primitive. As Joseph Campbell (1988) has pointed out, this required the suspension of a tendency toward empathy. Empathy was strictly reserved for in-groupers only.

Such a position prevails in present day us-them groups. The inherent logic of this position suggests that one's group is diminished in power by helping out-groupers. What one wants is power and, if possible, self sufficiency (see also Haidt, 2012).

Individuals and groups, on the other hand, who have moved to the inclusive position have as their goal inclusion rather than power. One seeks to welcome others instead of controlling them. Different individuals and groups are seen as bringing unique and diverse skills and awareness to the whole. Thus by inclusion the whole is made more capable. In this position the capacity to empathy is paramount. Cooperation is central between elements rather than competition.

All of this becomes a problem when us-them and inclusion groups attempt to work together, as in the recent U.S. Congress. Such a situation becomes troubled largely, because the us-them group holds as a major value a steadfast defense of its own position. It is not willing to cooperate with or become one of the larger group. It, if you will, doesn't know how to play well with others.

This is the case, because the us-them matrix requires "us" to prevail over "them." The only thing us-them groups are set up to accomplish is battle. And inclusion, it must be said, is not a battle tactic.

The typical way this clash ends is either with the us-them group conquering the includers and suppressing them--as is the case in a dictatorship. Any deviance from the us-position is severely dealt with. Dissent is dangerous. Another possibility is that the inclusion group grows and develops to the point it contains a pronounced majority. This situation presents a difficult situation for the us-them group as, instead of being battled, the inclusion group simply leaves the us-them group to its own increasingly isolated devices. That is, the us-them group is designed and set up for battle. If everyone simply goes away instead of battling, the main survival tactic becomes useless. In this case, the us-them group becomes an outlying minority position without effective input into the larger context.

Contemporary American political contrasts related to these issues have been articulated by Edsall (2012):

> Conservatives, argues researcher Philip Tetlock [see Tetlock 1983] of the Wharton School at the University of Pennsylvania, are less tolerant of compromise; see the world in "us" versus "them" terms; are more willing to use force to gain an advantage; are "more prone to rely on simple (good vs. bad) evaluative rules in interpreting policy issues;" are "motivated to punish violators of social norms (e.g., deviations from traditional norms of sexuality or responsible behavior [i.e., "morality"]) and to deter free riders."

Edsall described the results of a series of questions asked to conservative and liberal groups by the Pew Research Organization.

Findings show how profound the chasm is on values questions between liberals and conservatives. Generally speaking, not only do liberals place high importance on peace, mutual understanding, and empathy for those who have difficulty prevailing in competition, they demonstrate concern for equality of outcome, while conservatives place pointedly low or negative importance on such values. On the other side, conservatives believe that the use of force is a legitimate method of conflict resolution across a range of domains, from war to law enforcement to the discipline of children. Conservatives are more likely to believe in an "eye for an eye," are more likely to respect received tradition, and are overwhelmingly committed to the proposition that individuals are responsible for their own economic condition – all views rejected by liberals.

Nor, apparently, are these views open to easy discussion. Krugman (2012) cited views of Mooney concerning the futility of education (and presumably reason) in loosening Republican intransience:

For Republicans, having a college degree didn't appear to make one any more open to what scientists have to say. On the contrary, better-educated Republicans were more skeptical of modern climate science than their less educated brethren. Only 19 percent of college-educated Republicans agreed that the planet is warming due to human actions, versus 31 percent of non-college-educated Republicans.

In response, Krugman argued education and reason would not be effective with this group:

> What Chris Mooney is telling us is that this is a vain hope. Highly educated political conservatives--and this includes conservative economists--are going to be *less* persuadable by empirical evidence than the man or woman in the street. The more holes you poke in doctrines like expansionary austerity or supply-side economics, the more committed they will get to those doctrines.
>
> This debate isn't going to be won by rational argument.

What Krugman is seeing here is that evidence, debate, the presentation of options, &c. are ineffective in dealing with an us-them position. A big part of the reason this is true is related to how the us-them position is established. In this view *any-*

thing external to the position currently held is considered "other." Outside or other input will be repelled. That is, the rejection of such positions and input has more in common with a psychological defense than with a logical or empirical argument.

This is why "talking to someone" with whom you have a conflict may or may not work. Arguing with a defense, a dogma, or a fundamentalist position is futile as therapists in training learn.

Said Mooney (2012):

> As the new research suggests, conservatism is largely a defensive ideology -- and therefore, much more appealing to people who go through life sensitive and highly attuned to aversive or threatening aspects of their environments. By contrast, liberalism can be thought of as an exploratory ideology -- much more appealing to people who go through life trying things out and seeking the new.

In addition to this line of reasoning, another feature to be considered is that the diversity position is more intellectually and emotionally demanding than is the us-them position. Nuanced gray positions are harder to grasp and understand than obvious back and white logic. The progression from black and white to abstract gray thinking mirrors the range of intelligence capacity from low to high in much the same way as the capacity to integrate complexity and nuance indicates a more developed psychological functioning level.

Since rational argument and learning won't work, what will? It would seem any improvement in the situation requires a direct experience of a different context. This is why transformation has had such a significant history. Typically when you learn something the base does not shift. In a transformation, on the other hand, it is precisely the base that shifts. It is the nature of a transformation that things are seen from a different angle. Also, the more pronounced the base shift, typically the more profound the transformation.

Fear of change is not an effective survival tactic in the constantly evolving world we have. Flexibility and adaptability typically fare much better.

Appreciating and understanding complexity and nuanced "gray" positions requires a modicum of abstract reasoning ability as well as a developed grasp of the grammar of the language. Feeling comfortable with post-modern logic is the opposite of adhering rigidly to a rule.

That said, people in the world will always approximate a normal distribution. Range of capacity is not going to go away. There must be an honorable place for all. But how does one even conceive of such a welcoming place? The lowest common denominator? A system of severe laws to keep everyone in line? A diverse culture with groups of sub categories in which people may find a welcoming niche?

If all one has known is an us-them matrix, one has, by definition, not experienced a wide reaching acceptance. One has lived in an adversarial world. Effective experience in a diverse, empathic context allows a feeling of well being *simply for being oneself.* This is different from a sense of well-being coming from adherence to the right position or group.

If one is okay regardless of position or characteristics, there is no need to oppose all others. Further, such a state would be a continued evolution from the position of the survival of the group as seen with primitive person.

Having said that, this is not a solution that can be imposed. Imposing positions, anyway, is the wrong way to go. Besides, as Camus (1995) suggested, nirvana will not occur. But improvement can.

One way this can happen is to find ways to reward acts of empathy and inclusion. If such things become valuable, it is likely they will increase. This is the method one uses to teach a pigeon to peck a key in an experimental chamber. Over time it is possible inclusion will develop as a more central principle for more people.

The more psychologically secure one's base is, the more capable one is in facing the feared guardians at the gate who must be passed to get from the world of what is known to the world of what lies beyond what is known. An ability to withstand this fear is critical to the development of a more widespread inclusion. That is, if all one knows is one's own place, one does not even know that. This is true as one has no experiential context in which to place one's own place. One has an internal, but not an external, view.

Much of this effort has been hindered in the past by the wide reach of warring tribes. For example, religions have competed to be the true religion. Countries and cities have competed to be the most significant. Battles are carried on between rival theories.

Campbell called the one who crosses beyond the border of the known context "the Hero." This, in my opinion, was an unfortunate choice of word as it excludes too many travelers--not to mention creating a stereotyped masculine bias. I would have preferred it if he had used the world "seeker." The one who is "open to new experience" according to the Five Factor Model of Personality (see McCrae and John). "Little Mouse" will do (Storm, 1972).

Campbell (1949) labeled the impulse to cross the border to another context: "the call to adventure." This is something that can occur at any time.

> ...whether small or great, and no matter what the stage or grade of life, the call rings up the curtain, always, on a mystery of transfiguration--a rite, or moment, or spiritual passage, which, when complete, amounts to a dying and a birth. The familiar life horizon has been outgrown; the old concepts, ideals, and emotional pat-terns don't fit; the time for the passing of a threshold is at hand (p. 51).

Campbell saw this juncture in largely spiritual terms. It needn't be. It can be as mundane as flying from New York to Paris. Still such a juncture is difficult as it reawakens a deep-seated unconscious fear.

Freud has suggested that all moments of anxiety reproduce the
painful feelings of the first separation from the mother—the tighten-
ing of the breath, congestion of the
blood, etc., of the crisis of birth.
Conversely, all moments of separation and new birth create anxiety
(p. 52).

There is also a profound consequence to be discovered if the call to experience the unknown is
ignored--that is if one remains in the known context and defends it against any (even unknown)
options.

Refusal of the summons coverts
the adventure into its negative.
Walled in boredom, hard work, or
"culture," the subject loses the
power of significant affirmative
action and becomes a victim to be
saved. His flowering world becomes a wasteland of dry stones
and his life feels meaning-less--

> even though, like King Minos, he
> may through titanic effort succeed
> in building an empire of renown (p.
> 59).

Thus when growth and expansion is not pursued, all that remains is to fortify the present. And again this situation finds grounding in psychoanalysis.

> One is bound in by the walls of
> childhood; the father and mother
> stand as threshold guardians, and the
> timorous soul, fearful of some pun-
> ishment, fails to make the passage
> through the door and come to birth in
> the world without (p. 62).

In a rapidly evolving and changing world, espe-cially one in which distance has been shrunk al-most to the point of disappearing, diversified ca-pability is increasingly essential—not the rigid defense of one position or group against the rest. The essential truths are truths of all people, everywhere. A "seeker" can be male, female, old, young, Italian, South African, whatever. A seeker pursues that which lies beyond, not only in the transcendent sector, but in any beyond. The center that may serve as a base for the grounding of the self becomes (at least) the world instead of it being this neighborhood.

If different experiences are genuine in their own sense, they are part of who we are as human beings. In this sense, who we are is to be discovered through multiple experiences. The future lies beyond us. Similarly, an understanding of who we are lies in the reflection of what we experience beyond us as well.

THE PROBLEM OF POWER

The description of diversity thinkers as those who tend to be curious and interested in the new contrasts with the description of us-them thinkers as operating primarily from a position of fear. The fear position valorizes what I have now over what

210

I don't have. Such a zero-sum outlook opposes an outlook that seeks inclusion

An example is the following:

The Republican Party of Texas's 2012 platform has a plank on "Knowledge-Based Education" that reads:

> We oppose the teaching of Higher Order Thinking Skills (HOTS) (values clarification), critical thinking skills and similar programs that are simply a relabeling of Outcome-Education (OBE) (mastery learning) which focus on behavior modification and have the purpose of challenging the student's fixed beliefs and undermining parental authority (Rosenthal, 2012).

This difference echoes Klein's (see Hinshelwood, 1989, 1993) distinction between the "paranoid-schizoid" position and the "depressive" position. Here, persons displaying the paranoid-schizoid position routinely worry about who or what is going to hurt them. Those who display the depressive position, on the other hand, routinely worry about who they might hurt.

Developmentally, the first is considered more primitive than the second. That is the thought, "What's in it for me?" is considered to be more primitive than "We're all in this together." ("We're all bozos on this bus.") The difference between these groups might be called the split between the "me" and "us" groups. Obviously, then, this is a bit of an asymmetrical difference.

Power in the us-them group is routinely an attempt to consolidate power for me at the expense of you. Thus the stronger I get, the weaker you get, and the more power there is for me. The diversity group does not as a rule seek for power as such but seeks capability--in an attempt to increase capacity for all. Here leadership doesn't so much dictate as assist. That is, in this situation, the better each one does, the better we all do.

These "ways of seeing" become characteristics of groups, and they continually come into collision as the history of the world progresses. This is true, because the context is always changing as the culture develops and adapts to evolving realities of life and capacity for experience. By definition the "new" is "different." In an us-them view, different is "them." Such reasoning provides a strong impetus to resist change in favor of keeping things the same as they are now. By contrast, curiosity and an interest in the new is likely to welcome change and find it interesting and/or exciting.

Still time marches on though power may be mounted to resist it. A drive for power has haunted the human race throughout its history and has been responsible for horrendous cruelty.

If people have experienced adequate empathic resonance as children in order to develop a secure sense of self and attachment pattern, they have an internal referent to rely upon in navigating daily dilemmas. If, as so many, they have not developed an adequate and positive sense of self, it must be compensated for externally. Thus if one doesn't have an endoskeleton, one requires an exoskeleton. This is the situation in the U.S. where behavior is constrained primarily by external laws.

There isn't enough internal stability upon which to rely.

Foucault (1970) argued that viewpoints are reflective of the times in which they arise. A large part of the consequences of this can be understood in light of the inside view-outside view distinction. It may be said that an inside view and an outside view are never the same. This is why elements of, say, the Fourteenth Century can seem odd to our eyes, whereas they seemed quite normal to the eyes caught up in that time. One's own need to subtly distort reality in the service of self esteem or self justification apply primarily to the self. Others (outsiders) may not have this requirement and can therefore see oneself more objectively. (Of course these others will have their own distortions as well--which is why those in the Fourteenth Century, for example, could see some forms of oddness but not others.)

While multiple viewpoints might not be ideal for all purposes, they are at least more widely representative. Of course the views we have in this century are "this century's views" and therefore limited in similar fashion to the ways Fourteenth Century views were limited to the Fourteenth Cen-

214

tury.   Further, problems and limitations in our views are as invisible to us as errors in the Four- teenth Century views were to people of that time.

Us versus them positions sidestep the notions of accuracy and truth in favor of considerations of whether views are with us or not.   In this sense, determining position is easier than determining truth value. Further allegiance to the group can be demanded and subject to power in enforcement. Deviations from group loyalty or policy can be policed, and "deviants" can be punished. Purity of rank tends to rise in importance, and examinations of the sensibility of group claims tends to lose im- portance.

On the other hand, diversity of view tends to widen the scope of interest.   Seeking divergent views that might modify currently held positions decreases rigidity as well as the establishment of doctrinaire positions. Also, since the fate of every view is to have a newer interpretation, exploration of difference helps enable the future.

All of this is, of course, made possible by the nature of reality as well as the logic of the lan- guage we use to understand that reality.   These features prevent a hopeless relativity and inability to understand others. It is not, as a rule, the nature of reality nor the logic of language that changes. It is the cultural influences that force ontologies. That is, emotional investments, breadth of viewpoints, degree of complex and abstract abilities, &c. help determine the array of possible understandings that may be made. Fausto-Sterling (2000), for example, showed how sexual prejudice informed and distorted scientific explorations of sex hormones. We see what our contexts allow us to see. In order to see more, we need a different context. It is this fact that ultimately tends to confine us to one age.

Thus the male context tends to differ from the female context just as the German context tends to differ from the Japanese. The two may come together in yet a third context called "both." But each will likely bring different strengths to "both." Seen in this light it is interesting that the academic study of a field benefits from open, high bandwidth approaches. But professional accreditation and standards tend to be more black or white absolutes. The very best minds are thus sometimes required to toe the lines like slaves (an us-them position).

The collision between excitement for the new versus fear of it is a force in the culture that fractures cooperation, effort devoted toward progress, human well-being, compassion, and genuine personhood. It is in our way. The "versus" part has to go. These extremes need to be assimilated as "parts of the group." And the hatred and killing must stop. It has been too long.

I heard somewhere that Americans fall generally into one or another of four different groups. The groups are: 1) intellectual and cultural, 2) business, 3) workers, and 4) disenfranchised. Of course there is infinite inner-group variation, but in general the focus of these groups is different. Groups are classified by the kinds of matters that are the modal focus of those in each group. Furthermore, the goal of each group is different. That is, they differ in what they wish to have more of. Culture and learning? Money and monetary power? An enjoyable, full life? Escape?

In light of these considerations, it has always been an American myth that if one is enterprising enough, one can make it to the top--whatever the top is considered to be in one's group. A house painter may develop a network of house painting operations. Such a person may make a good deal of money. And this may be considered "making it" in his or her region. Someone may get his or her novel published by a prestigious house, and people may say he or she has "made it." Someone may become CEO of his or her company. This may be considered "making it." One may even win the lottery.

Just as certainly, of course, publishing a well selling book, becoming a CEO, having a great group of friends, or winning the lottery will not always be considered important in other sectors.

For the most part, those who show intellectual and cultural talent tend to come from homes in which intellectual and cultural talent is prized-- likely beyond all other things. Similarly those who succeed in business often have business ori- ented families and friends. Factory workers likely had factory worker parents. And welfare people often came from welfare homes.

I am trying to make two points here: 1) Family experience tends to create an ontology, and 2) it is difficult to have profound experience of multiple ontologies.

The result of this is that excellence in groups tends to proliferate along group lines. This is definitely NOT to say that all the bright students are enrolled in Ivy League schools. Clearly they are not. Many a gem, it is said, can be found at the whistle stop. Nor do stunning business performances occur only to those who are schooled and inbred to business. (Think, for example, of Albert Einstein in reference to the first point and Steve Jobs in reference to the second.)

Barak Obama's mother pointed him toward academic achievement since he was a child. But she was a spectacular academic herself.

The notion of power has to do with hierarchy. Those with more power have certain capabilities those without power are denied. The extreme example of this is an autocratic arrangement. Here the power is constellated in the leader, to whom others are subservient. Such a situation raises the question of voice. Who is heard? In the most extreme cases the autocrat is heard and others are not. This situation is opposed by a situation in which every voice is heard.

Further, since it is a critical ingredient in abuse that one's voice does not get to count, autocracy becomes an abusive situation. The more every voice is allowed to be heard, the less abuse there will be in a system. That is levels of abuse are a function of percentages of power. Yet allowing all voices to be heard (and genuinely considered) does not necessarily reduce them all to the same level or significance. Some voices will naturally be more significant than others for a variety of reasons.

This need not be an inherent problem, however, in a context when power is held to a minimum. In such a situation, a place must be found for every voice regardless of its eloquence or lack thereof. Any solution will be a solution for the group as a whole.

When power is injected into the situation, the element of winning and losing is injected along with it. With the abandonment of a goal of equality, domination enters the equation (Benjamin, 1988). That is if I seek to dominate you, I erase you. If I seek to submit to you, I erase me. With power comes erasure. This has been the routine character of developing cultures of the world.

Various groups have been set up in a power position: landowners, wealthy people, men, politicians, professors, and some parents--to consider a few. It has seemed quite normal for such people to dominate others. But this has not led to a widely prosperous society nor a highly humane one.

The power position reaches all the way to satire in the case of the legendary European petty official. Once in Lisbon, I found myself on Sunday without adequate money. There were no ATMs in that time, so it occurred to me I could get some cash at the money change booth at the airport. When I got there, I was met by the "keeper of the gate." This man told me, "You can't enter unless you have a ticket." I explained I just wanted to go to the lobby to get some money. No way. No ticket; no entrance.

Rebuffed, I started to walk away. (There was no arguing with this person.) At that moment I remembered I did have a plane ticket--but it was for a flight that left from Luxembourg, an entirely different country, in a month. "Worth a try," I thought.

I returned to the man, who was very wary seeing me approach. "I have a ticket" I said and showed him my ticket.

"Oh, ticket," he said and gestured for me to pass.

Now I can understand that keeping undesirables, such as tourists, out of the airport was important. But who, I wondered, thought up this procedure? What did it really accomplish?

The impulse to rise above others in order to feel superior to them is different from the impulse to do one's best in the hopes it will benefit the entire group. That is, benefiting others does not obviate achievement. Achievement is a contribution in such a case. It is not achievement against.

Governing rules and regulations must consider the voices of those regulated in order to contribute to the well being of the whole. Imposed rules and regulations that deny voices are damaging to cultural well-being. It is important that the way to the future be more humane or it may not reflect well on our capabilities as a species.

REFERENCES

Banjamin, J. The Bonds of Love: psychoanalysis, feminism, and the problem of domination. Pantheon. 1988.

Campbell, J. The Hero with a Thousand Faces. Princeton. 1949.

Campbell, J. The Inner Reaches of Outer Space: metaphor as myth and as religion. Harper. 1988.

Camus, A. Resistance, Rebellion, and Death: Essays. Vintage. 1995.

Edsall, T.B. "Conservatives vs. liberals: more than politics." Huffington Post. 02-08-12.

Fausto-Sterling, A. Sexing the Body: gender politics and the construction of sexuality. Basic. 2000.

Foucault, M. The Order of Things: an archaeology of the human sciences. Random House. 1970.

Haidt, J. "Forget the Money, Follow the Sacredness." New York Times. 03-17-2012.

Hinshelwood, R. A Dictionary of Kleinian Thought, Free Association. 1989.

Hinshelwood, R. Clinical Klein, Free Association. 1993.

Krugman, P. "This tribal nation." New York Times. 02-27-2012.

McCrae R.R. and John, O.P. "An introduction to the Five-Factor Model and Its Applications." http://psych.colorado.edu/~carey/Courses/PSY-C5112/Readings/psnBig5_Mccrae03.pdf

Mooney, C. "Want to understand Republicans? First understand evolution." Huffington Post. 02-08-12.

Rosenthal, A. "No comment necessary: Texas GOP's 2012 platform opposes teaching "critical thinking skills." New York Times. 06-29-12.

Storm, H. Seven Arrows. Harper. 1972.

Tetlock, P.E. "Cognitive style and political ideology," *Journal of Personality and Social Psychology* 45 (1983): 118-26,

I have discovered one of these internalized contexts operative in my own life. When I was little, my parents, and especially my mother, were so concerned with their own needs and wishes concerning me that there was no room left for my own wishes and needs. I remember quite young I came to the feeling that my mother was battling my perceptions and thoughts, because they posed threats to her own. She wanted to script everything about me, so I would be the person she wanted me to be instead of allowing me to discover the person I actually was. The effect of this on me was that I felt that if I were to agree with my mother (which action pleased her no end), I would lose myself. Life in my childhood home became a war of whether or not my self would survive. I wanted to protect it, and she wanted to destroy it.

Also, as with other children, I longed most earnestly for that which I did not have. For me that was acceptance. In short, I felt crippled, because I did not have it. But I discovered others did. They had it, and I did not. I intimately came to know the difference between those who were able to accept others and those who battled. These were two different sectors defined by how much they could accept.

THE MORMONS

By midnight he had left the road
and the burning woods behind
him and had come out on the
highway once more. The moon,
riding low above the field beside
him, appeared and disappeared,
diamond-bright, between patch-
es of darkness.   Intermittently
the boy's jagged shadow slanted
across the road ahead of him as
if it cleared a rough path toward
his goal. His singed eyes, black
in their deep sockets, seemed
already to envision the fate that
awaited him but he moved
steadily on, his face set toward

the dark city, where the children
of God lay sleeping.

--Flannery O'Connor
The Violent Bear It Away

I grew up in Utah. This meant I was surrounded
by Mormons. I have tried to understand what this
means all my life. Let me say Mormons are not as
a rule the best group to live among--especially if
you are not one of them.

It is, however, now clear to me that in the area
where I lived as a child, Mormon beliefs were routinely conflated with the unsophisticated and un-
worldly views of the (mostly) working class local
residents. Further a good number of these people
had quite rigid ideas and tended to see the world in
black and white terms. Politically they tended to
be far right, and their lives, with notable excep-
tions, did not center on much beyond the Mormon
Church.

That is to say, these were people who, as a rule, were not so much focused on a search for what might be new and different. They were more commonly organized around polarizing the world into subsections of "us versus them"--and experiencing reality as a battle between these two.

I was different from the start.

Topologically or nominally at least I was not a complete "other." A major alien. My great grandmother had walked across the plains with the Mormon Pioneers. I knew her before she died. My mother's father was the marshal of Bountiful, Utah, and my mother was in some minute degree still Mormon, though much of that influence had left her in college. My father was a sometime Methodist from Indiana as well as being of good German stock. He was not a religious person, though he was a 32nd degree Mason.

Neither of my parents attended church.

Rare for my neighborhood, both my parents were university-trained professionals. My father was an electrical engineer at Utah Power and

231

Light Company (now Pacific Power), and my mother taught at the University of Utah.

Whatever ties I was able to profess that I had to the Mormons, though, did not seem to be enough. The (mostly us-them) Mormons, I was quick to learn, liked to stay to themselves and also distance themselves from non Mormons. Further, where I lived, there were enough Mormons that they had considerable influence on political and civic affairs.

Their impact on my life began more extensively when I went to grade school. Virtually all my classmates were Mormon. Usually this did not present too much of a problem at school. We all got to be pals, and the biggest contrast between us was whether or not we were athletic. This situation could change, however, when we got home. My friends' parents were not always at ease with me. Some treated me with coolness, over-management, or would not let their kids play with me.

Once I even heard I was "of the Devil."

Me. I was the little kid who took piano lessons. "Of the Devil." Whatever that means.

Since virtually all my school friends went to the Mormon Church, I wanted to go too. I sat through the meetings and even went to Sunday School. None of these were very inspiring, as Mormon Church services tend to resemble business meetings--often with some conservative moralism thrown in for good measure.

The one thing I did learn is that the main emphasis was on *obedience*. This was the most important thing for sure. I also remember hearing, "When the prophet has spoken, the argument is over." The thing to do was to comply.

In the meantime, my friends and I were growing; we were people. Consequently we were interested in school, and, at least for me, school was a more important environment than church. In fact, school was the place we each could begin to find *contrast*. Like other ghettos, Utah was largely composed of one influence only. There was, if you will, only one tune on the iPhone. In school we learned what lay beyond this.

Aside from school for us and work for the adults, Mormonism was a major focus. It was the ground, the very stuff of life. Further, the Mormons were always stressing the fact they were *right*. This meant a great deal to them. Even in those pre-postmodern times, being right had the heft of a raison d'être.

Not being a Mormon was always a factor with which I felt I had to struggle. It *always* mattered. I was okay, you know, but I would have been so much better without my flaw. The early grades in school weren't too bad. We were all learning how to be around each other, to be part of a group. Of course there was always a "hard core" cluster of religiously influenced kids that was quite rigid with its boundaries of which person it would and would not include.

In middle school we were trying to figure out what to do with sex and the weirdness that was happening to our bodies. There was, again, some exclusivity, but the big deal in school still was athletics. In high school, the gap began to widen. The Mormon kids routinely became student body officers. They dated each other. If one were not Mormon, there was often no real use dating you. Mormons were determined to pair up with other Mormons.

It was even explained to me once that interaction of Mormons with non-Mormons was ideally to be restricted to activities designed to convert "them."

This meant there were some (otherwise) wonderful kids who were off-limits or largely off limits to the Mormons. And it must be said there were, as well, some Mormon kids who befriended me as well as others and made those like me feel welcome. But the stigma was ever-present--to a lesser or greater degree--in the airwaves at school. Non-Mormon was definitely second-class.

This binary was hugely broken down at the university--even at the University of Utah. It persisted for the Mormons, but at the university, the Mormon kids had no particular advantage. You could, for example, be non-Mormon and score higher.

Further, the goal of a liberal education is to examine the intellectual and cultural accomplishments of multiple viewpoints. In this enterprise, rigidity began to be an impediment. And the toll was highest for the least supple of students. I heard a million times believers say that Mormons have the truth, so they don't need to learn anything else.

This is actually a much more disastrous view than it sounds at first, because if all I know is one thing, I don't know the context in which that one thing exists. That is to say, I am trapped in an "inside view." An "inside view" and an "outside view" are never the same. Knowing one thing keeps me from knowing where my one things stands in the whole. I literally don't know where I am.

Also, at the university, professors--as professors are wont--tended to regard rigidity with less than rapture. That was when I left my hometown.

The problem was though I was through with it; it was not through with me.

Throughout this early period of my experience there were people who were friendly and kind in one form or another. They may have had strong notions about things, but at least they tried to help and encourage people to see the value in such notions. But there were others who exerted an authoritarian sort of certainty. These latter people appeared punitive, as was the Deity they imagined. Essentially, if you followed their notions, you were okay. If, on the other hand, you deviated, you were a problem. The worst possible outcome was to be cast into "outer darkness."

And that was as bad as it sounds.

Further, the idiocy one was required to support and follow allowed little questioning. No. This was "holy writ." Such positions came straight from the Deity to those in charge--who appeared to be inflated with a feeling of inevitability at directing others. That was their job.

Of course it must be said, Mormons raised outside Utah are routinely themselves in the minority, so the experiences I had are similar in some ways to theirs. And majorities may either be open or defensive.

It has always struck me Mormon leaders are called "authorities." This may conjure warmth in your mind, but it goes in a different direction in mine. Further, these "authorities" busy themselves with being unassailable. That is, they claim to have the correct answers. These are to be accepted simply because the "authority" said so.

I did not see anyone openly question anything. If one disagreed, one kept one's mouth shut. Either that, or one risked unpleasant consequences. My friends even largely sought to wear the same clothes. And though the "authorities" typically had not studied any alternative to their views and approach in much detail, they were convinced--and convinced us--anything else was inadequate, or more to the point: wrong.

The result of this treatment was a climate of fear. People toed the line, as there were serious--even eternal--consequences for not doing so. It was a militaristic sort of autocracy. At any cost the Deity must be pleased in order to avoid negative consequences.

I began to develop a certain sort of incredulity about this Mormon Deity. Essentially the figure appeared to have laid down the "proper path." Everyone was encouraged to follow this path. It was the key to realizing glory. The Mormons were always talking about how loving this deity was. But, like a dysfunctional father, the Deity was most loving to those who did what he liked. The others were in perpetual need of help if not outright prodding. This was not a Deity to be taken lightly.

Further this was not a Deity interested in having you remain who you really were. Mormon children were taught to play the game (follow the path). They were taught to "get it right." There was little stress on "getting it real"--especially if one's real impulse was away from Mormonism.

In other words, the more one gets it right and becomes a "good kid" (instead of being the "real kid") [the "real (rotten) kid?"] the more one is rewarded. Further the right kid is the one who gets to go to church, to school, to grow and develop. The goal seemed to be that one would adopt the right self as one's essential identity. The real self was best left behind, as the deity was not interested in that one.

The devout provided a template of what a "good person" would look like. One's task was to approximate that template. That's what the Deity wanted. Choose the right.

This template included being clean, well groomed, generally happy, obedient, positive, and "wholesome." Especially to be avoided were drinking coffee, smoking, any form of swearing, or most especially: sex.

This is essentially good training for a robot. If the Bishop was an ass, one had better get it right instead of getting it real and smile and nod while he spoke. Getting it real and (correctly) identifying him as an ass would get one in deep grief.

This kind of approach is practically the definition of dysfunctionality. Typical human interchange is abandoned in the service of avoiding censure from a judging parent. It is the primary climate of abuse. There is always a problem when one is denied a voice. In this case one is effectively denied a voice if having one leads to retribution and isolation.

To one outside the dysfunction, the arrangement routinely appears odd if not intolerable. To one inside it is a survival situation requiring careful maneuvering--odd looking or not. It is only when a way out has been found--where one can survive as who one really is, voice and all--that one has a hope of moving from being right to being real. Only then can the happy face be lowered.

In this sense if the Deity lost "his" power to disapprove, Mormonism would fall apart. (There would be no reason to comply, and everyone would be welcome.)

Many, many people in my background gradually learned to play the game. They got it right. Then they found someone else who was also right, and contracted the right sort of marriage. This was a rite undertaken in a Mormon Temple. Such a rite married one for "time and all "eternity." (Lord save us.) A "mere" civil service only married one for time.

Then the couple was urged by the Mormon culture to immediately have children, and have as many as they could. They were, of course, to continue their devotion to the religion. Work assignments ("callings") were designed to keep people busy and focused on the church. Then the cycle was completed again.

People were urged to avoid out-of-church activities and exposure, as "Satan" lurked "out" there with the express intent of luring souls into the "evil" of contemporary culture--or worse: the study of philosophy, sex, or, even Catholicism.

There were three major results of this approach (us-them). First, the life-style of the Mormons was, by and large, sharply different from that of non-Mormon people. Mingling was awkward in many cases. Second, because of their engulfment in their own culture, many Mormons were denied access to what might be called the "American experience." That is an experience with American diverse acceptance at its base, instead of an experience of one group set off from the many. And, at a fundamental level, the Mormon habit of accepting pronouncements as truth, left high-level academic and intellectual thinking routinely in conflict. Such thinking could be engaged, but only after the religion had been safely compartmentalized apart.

(Recently at a playground in Prospect Park, Brooklyn, where I was playing with my grandson, these thoughts came to me. Here we were surrounded by all manner of people, rich, poor, different races, cultures--and all of us were having a terrific time. The prevailing mood was definitely one of acceptance. How different, I thought, had been the divisive experience I felt in Utah. That sensibility seemed a million miles away.)

I didn't experience very much of adult Mormon life. By the time I got to the university, and many of my high school peers were getting married and going to work, I basically transferred from a Mormon to an academic context. It was so different! I fell in love with it.

It is not that Mormons don't go to college; they do. But the center of school is the core of academic exploration. The center of Mormonism is the doctrine. The two are different in many essential ways--as are the American and Mormon experiences. The academic center is an accumulation of history's achievements and studies. The Mormon center is comprised of adherence to the dogma and the "revealed" truths.

After high school, a good number of Mormon kids go on missions for the church. These are two-year affairs in which young men and women are placed all over the world to proselytize the LDS religion. This experience tends to significantly strengthen one's bond with the religion.

(Though one of my patients told me the first time he dropped acid was on his LDS mission.)

When one returns, one is expected to marry as soon as possible and start a family. There is a concerted effort to keep the church in the center of life of its members when they are adults as well.

What I do know about adult Mormon experience is that it is very involved. The adults work to maintain church affairs and to provide "approved" experiences for their children. There is a high degree of (traditionally defined) family involvement in the religion. The religion continues to be the focal point of most activity. Adults walk or drive to church in their dresses, suits, and ties. Men and women carry copies of "the scriptures" with them. Appearing to belong is a big deal to these people, and they go a long way to cultivate this appearance.

Kids grow. They date and marry--in the Mormon Church of course. Their parents attend. The grandparents remain highly involved in the lives of their children and their grandchildren--to the exclusion of other enterprises. When someone dies, there is a Mormon funeral. The Mormon funeral is its own thing.

Depending on location these are traditionally held in a church house and involve speakers and brief musical offerings. The speakers relate what a wonderful person so-and-so was and manage to recite a few humorous antidotes about him or her. This is almost an obligatory format. And central to the speech will be comments about how so-and-so is in a "much better place." Essentially a Mormon funeral is supposed to be a mix of sadness and happiness. The deceased has "risen" to live in glory and perpetuity. So-and-so's good fortune is celebrated as much as the congregation's loss.

In this way the present is seen as a preparatory period for the crucial future.

Additionally, the Mormon Church is now, and as best I can tell, has always been interested in power. This is usually more or less covered up with "niceness." Nonetheless, Mormons have a history of striving to be independent rather than joining. They are only nominally Americans. They once even prepared to fight the U.S. Army. They have their own society, and it is critical to preserve that.

The Mormons have a saying that one should be "*in* the world, not *of* the world."

Don't join with anyone.

This has resulted in a long history of conflict between Mormons and everyone else. Repeatedly run out of several locations for an inability or refusal to get along with their neighbors, Mormons sought to grab up all the power in Utah. This would keep other influences at bay.

To this day, the Utah Legislature is routinely overloaded with fundamentalist Mormons. In my time this was associated with the Republican Party. The legislating of morality was always a main concern. As was a fierce resistance to going along with federal regulations that were opposed locally. The highly conservative legislature functions to preserve the LDS hegemonic influence in Utah. And, it might be said, does pretty well at this (see Gorrell, 2011).

The Mormons say they are "adhering to a higher standard," but what it really turns out to be is a more restricted as well as isolated standard.

PART II

In order to understand these themes, experiences, and tendencies I took up a brief study of Mormon history as well as a study of its significant leaders: Joseph Smith and Brigham Young. Such a study is not at all as easy as it might sound. Although there is an extensive literature about the Mormons, most of it is apology--and that is clearly designed to defend the church as well as attempting to put it in a positive light. There is also another large literature devoted to attacking the church. Virtually none of this is helpful to genuine study.

In between these two trends there is a much smaller body of work that attempts to adhere to academic standards of scholarship. That is, these are studies that attempt to rely on objective evidence, logical reasoning, and printed historical record--in similar fashion to academic works focusing on other topics.

This scholastic literature is routinely besieged by apologists and attackers. Clearly it is important that it be found wanting. Still, a brief survey of this literature yields a plausible outline of events.

The Mormon Church began when Joseph Smith, a poor, uneducated, young man claimed to have discovered some golden plates and "translated them" to produce The Book of Mormon. Joseph was born in 1805. The only existing account of his childhood is that of his mother, an account that was later suppressed by Brigham Young (Anderson, 1999, p. 2). The New England family struggled at farming and moved several times in Joseph's youth, eventually ending up around Palmyra in upper New York State.

It was then the frontier, and life was difficult. There was little education, and the religious tenor was still that of Jonathan Edwards, with his spiders and bricks. Joseph's mother's parents were considered nonconformist, and both Joseph's parents were unsettled in religion (Ibid, p.3). His father was fond of witchcraft and magic (Ibid, p. 16). Fearing available religions were corrupted, Joseph's parents longed for what they considered to be the "lost primitive church."

Joseph grew up on a religious frontier as well. Many doctrines were being espoused, and conversions were frequent, if short lived. In Joseph's family dreams and visions were interchangeable. There was no grounding in current science, logic, or learned matters. Such frontier people would surely have been overwhelmed by St. Peters Basilica in Rome, completed about two hundred years earlier.

Actually there was rather intense anti-Catholic fever in Joseph's area at the time, though it is doubtful there were any reasonably scholastic Catholics in the area.

> The sober preacher trained in the dialectics of the seminary was rare west of the Appalachians. One found instead faith healers and circuit-rider evangelists, who stirred their audiences to paroxysms of religious frenzy...The settlers in the old Northwest Territory demanded personality rather than diplomas

from the men who called them to
God (Brodie, p. 13-14).

With essentially no grounding but current experience, the Smith family along with their neighbors were left to their own devices in a desperately primitive and difficult hand to mouth existence. These people basically lived on the dirt with scant protection from hunger, disease, or the elements.

In addition, there is evidence that Joseph's father was alcoholic, and his mother was seriously depressed. They lived in poverty and extreme need. Both Lucy's [Joseph's mother] parents had visions, and they were talked about in the Smith family (Anderson, p. 16, 20). A strong acceptance of magic came to the U.S. with the Pilgrims and magical practices were routine among the uneducated.

When Joseph was age eight, he developed typhoid fever. The fever cleared, but infection remained in his leg. At first it was thought amputation was necessary, but Joseph's mother strongly resisted this. Joseph was operated two times without anesthetic. This was apparently an horrendous procedure that left him forever with a limp (Brodie, p. 8). [Brodie is an eminent historian who is originally from Utah.]

Anderson (1999), a psychoanalyst, pointed out such massive early trauma would have a formative impact on the developing psychology of the young Joseph. It was overwhelming, with the surgeon in the position of the doer, and Joseph in the (helpless) position of the done to. Also, being left with a limp, left him with a "flaw." The ordeal of the operation and the recovery were certainly no fantasy, nor were they curable by fantasy, visions, or the supernatural. They were real.

Apparently the operation did not dampen the Smith family story telling, dreaming, or longing for capacities beyond what surrounded them. Besides, religious awakenings and arguments were popular in the area. Answers and options were sought. Following a bout with pneumonia, Lucy became hyper-religious. One imagines it was the only option available.

Joseph was his mother's favorite, and had little trouble replacing his father in his mother's affections, with--no doubt--the resulting Oedipal con-

sequences. This would have made it more difficult for Joseph to give up fantasized solutions in
favor of reality. It would also have tended to keep
him fixated at a more black or white level of interpretation.

It is not at all far-fetched to think that Joseph
experienced a conflict between who he really was:
a poor, unlearned, manipulator, and who he so
desperately desired to be: someone truly special.
Further, given his penchant for magic and appearance, it is not at all unreasonable that, rather than
put in the long years required to become a person
of ability, he simply put on the appearance he was
already there.

Psychologically, he developed an idealized false
self (all capable) to cover (and protect) the real
self (not worth much). He then progressively
identified with the false self. This is a pattern
known as narcissism. It is a kind of compensation
for profound feelings of inferiority.

Joseph certainly had much to feel inferior about.
His limp. The birth and death of his own de-
formed child. His lack of education. His crushing
poverty.

As his family and his real prospects were unable to support him, Joseph turned to magic, as was not altogether unusual at the time. Fantasy became his focus over reality. At age 13, he began using divining rods to search for treasure (Ibid, p. 22). At age 16 he was using seer stones (Brodie, p. 20). He sold his services to farmers in his area for the purposes of locating riches. It must be pointed out that in order to practice magic, one must deceive *both* oneself and another.

According to Brodie, Joseph's first accounted-for vision occurred when he was 17.

> It was the first time in my life that I had made such an attempt [going into a wood to "seek guidance of the Lord"], for amidst all my anxieties I had never as yet made the attempt to pray vocally...I kneeled down and began to offer up the desires of my heart to God. I had scarcely done so, when immediately I was seized upon by some power which entirely over-came me, and had such an astonish-

253

ing influence over me as to bind my tongue so that I could not speak. Thick darkness gathered around me, and it seemed to me for a time as if I were doomed to sudden destruction...just at this moment of great alarm, I saw a pillar of light over my head, above the brightness of the sun, which descended gradually until it fell upon me. It no sooner appeared than I found myself delivered from the enemy which held me bound. When the light rested upon me I saw two personages, whose brightness and glory defy all description, standing above me in the air. One of them spake unto me, calling me by name, and said--pointing to the other—

"This is my beloved Son, hearHim."

My object in going to inquire of the Lord was to know which of all the sects was right, and I might know which to join. No sooner, therefore, did I get possession of myself, so as to be able to speak, than I asked the personages who stood above me in the light, which of all the sects was right—and which I should join. I was answered that I must join none of them, for they were all wrong, and the personage who addressed me said that all their creeds were an abomination in His sight: that those professors were all corrupt; that "they draw near to me with their lips, but their hearts are far from me; they teach for doctrines the commandments of men; having a form of godliness, but they deny the power thereof." He again forbade me to join with any of them: and many other things did he say unto me, which I cannot write at this time. When I came to myself again, I]found myself lying on my back, looking up into heaven. (Brodie, p. 22)

In Joseph's autobiographical sketch of 1834, however, there was "no whisper of [this] event that, if it had happened, would have been the most soul-shattering experience of his whole youth (Brodie, p. 24)."

In a draft version of the vision dictated between 1831 and 1832, Joseph's account was different again as follows:

..in the 16th year of my age...the Lord opened the heavens upon me and I saw the Lord." By 1835 this had changed to a vision of two "personages" in "a pillar of fire" above his head, and "many angels." In the published version the personages had become God the Father and His son Jesus Christ, and the angels had vanished. Joseph's age had changed to fourteen (Brodie, p. 24).

Brodie (1946) pointed out that townspeople preferred the word "visions" to "lies." Visions were widely considered to be an escape from the rigors of current reality. And in this department, Joseph had considerable talent. Not only had he told complex stories and fantasies all his life to a family that highly approved, but his need to have fantasy supersede reality would have had considerable energy behind it.

Daniel Hendrix, who helped in setting the type for the printing of the Book of Mormon recalled:

> He was known among the young men I associated with as a romancer of the first water. I never knew so ignorant a man as Joe was to have such a fertile imagination. He could never tell a common occurrence in his daily life without embellishing the story with his imagination; yet I remember he was grieved one day when old Parson Reed told Joe that he was going to hell for his lying habits (Ibid, p. 26).

At age 21 Joseph was arrested, basically for fraud. He had gypped a farmer out of money to find treasure and failed (as usual). The case went to trial, and Joseph was publicly censured.

This would have been a blow to his idealized self. But that self was robust enough at the time, the events did not crush it. Joseph wrote:

> At the age of ten my father's family removed to Palmyra, New York, where and in the vicinity of which, I lived, or, made it my place of residence, until I was twenty-one; the latter part, in the town of Manchester. During this time, as is common to most or all youths, I fell into many vice and follies; but as my accusers are, and have been forward to accuse me of being guilty of gross and outrageous violations of the peace and good order of the community, I take the occasion to remark that, though, as I have said above, "as is common to most, or all youths, I fell into many vices and follies," I have not, neither can it be sustained, in truth, been guilty of wronging or injuring any man or society of men; and those imperfections to which I

allude, and for which I have often had occasion to lament, were a light, too often, vain mind, exhibiting a foolish and trifling conversation (Brodie, p. 17).

There are accounts from this time that Joseph's neighbors thought of him as "shiftless."

In the area around Palmyra there were several Indian burial mounds. There was a lively interest in their history. Following the ordeal of treasure seeking, Joseph got the idea he would write an history of the mound builders.

Joseph had another vision in his room at home in which he was told of the golden plates buried in the mound. Joseph's father believed this vision. Joseph claimed he had retrieved the plates and enlisted an enthusiastic neighboring farmer, Martin Harris to be his scribe as Joseph "translated" the plates from "reformed Egyptian." (A safe language, as this pre-dated the discovery of the Rosetta Stone.) Harris was to write down what Joseph dictated by looking into a hat that held his seer stone.

At this time only Harris and Joseph's family believed him. Harris' wife, however, was not pleased by this enterprise and sought to see the manuscript. Harris had transcribed 116 pages at that time. Finally Joseph acceded and Harris took the pages home with him for her to see. At this point the manuscript disappeared (Brodie, p. 54). It appears she destroyed it, as it has never been found. Joseph's mother wrote:

> "Oh, my God," Joseph cried. "All is lost! What shall I do?" He wept and groaned, and walked the floor continually, and after a while told Harris to go back and search once more. "No," he replied, "it is all in vain; for I have ripped open beds and pillows; and I know it is not there (see Lucy Mack Smith, 1853)."

This left Joseph in a dilemma. Clearly he could not duplicate the lost material. The solution he hit upon was not at all unusual for Joseph: he had a vision. Still, it seems the translation experience had deepened Joseph. He also had been developing a more religious focus.

This was Joseph's "explanation" upon the loss of the first manuscript (Brodie, p. 56).

TO THE READER—

As many false reports have been circulated respecting the following work, and also many unlawful measures taken by evil designing persons to destroy me, and also the work, I would inform you that I translated, by the gift and power of God, and caused to be written, one hundred and sixteen pages, the which I took from the Book of Lehi, which was an account abridged from the plates of Lehi, by the hand of Mormon; which said account, some person or persons have stolen and kept from me, notwithstanding my utmost exertions to recover it again--and being commanded of the

Lord that I should not translate the
same over again, for Satan had put
it into their hearts to tempt the Lord
their God, by altering the words,
that they did read contrary from that
which I translated and caused to be
written; and if I should bring forth
the same words again, or, in other
words, if I should translate the same
over again, they would publish that
which they had stolen, and Satan
would stir up the hearts of this generation that they might not receive
this work: but behold, the Lord said
unto me, I will not suffer that Satan
shall accomplish his evil design in
this thing: therefore thou shalt translate from the plates of Nephi, until
ye come to that which ye have
translated, which ye have retained;
and behold ye shall publish it as the
record of Nephi; and thus I will
confound those who have altered
my words, I will not suffer that they
shall destroy my work: yea, I will
shew unto them that my wisdom is
greater than the cunning of the Dev-

il. Where-fore, to be obedient unto the commandments of God, I have, through his grace and mercy, accomplished that which he hath commanded me respecting this thing. I would also inform you that the plates of which hath been spoken, were found in the town-ship of Manchester, Ontario county, New York

THE AUTHOR

Joseph's vision directed him to a second set of plates that held the material for a religious book (Ibid, p. 55). Joseph sought a neighbor named Oliver Cowdry to help him with this new "translation." He also hung a sheet between himself and Cowdry and gave up his seer stone in favor of a pair of stones from a breastplate, which he called the "Urim and Thumum." Joseph claimed to translate through these.

The product of this translation was the Book of Mormon, and Joseph founded his religion "The

Church of Christ" two weeks after its completion. He appointed himself President.

The Book of Mormon is essentially a chronicle of many wars. These pit obvious good guys against obvious bad guys. Including the story of the Jeredites (Brodie, p. 71), the Book of Mormon was formed in light of the opinions of the times current where Joseph lived. When he could not think of what to write, it seems he simply inserted verses from the Bible (but used only the King James translation--unavailable at the time the Bible was written).

According to the Doctrine and Covenants, a compilation of Joseph's writings and visions, Joseph included biblical quotes as he was clarifying and "fixing" them.

Brodie (p. 62) felt the Book of Mormon was a dull story of mediocre talent.

Anderson (1999) however felt the Book of Mormon was based on Joseph's own autobiography, told in allegorical and symbolic form. Using the device of applied psychoanalysis and psychobiography, Anderson reasoned that the speed of dictation of the Book of Mormon suggested a process akin to free association.

Seen through this lens, the Book of Mormon appears as a series of exploits in which Joseph symbolically seeks to triumph over his adversities. The surgeon's scalpel, for example, appears as the Sword of Laban (Ibid, p.43). Nephi represents Joseph's alter-ego (p. 44) in a family with power struggles. Nephi's victories are Joseph's compensation for his experience of helplessness during his terrible (life threatening) surgery. This is a way Joseph is able to symbolically triumph over terrible real life experiences with a conquering fantasy.

Being a conquering hero instead of a helpless victim, also supports the positive affective coloring of the idealistic self.

In the Book of Mormon there is routinely a simple conflation of power with "good." This may be thought to be a narcissistic fantasy. (It is simply not considered power could be bad.) In this sense the Book of Mormon becomes a book of intense division.

It is also a book in which there is virtually no place for women (Ibid, p. 178). The purpose of women seems to have been in having babies, cooking, and taking care of families. Women were, thus, those who supported the families while the men went to seek power in the religion.

It may be said that Joseph was attempting to conquer his personal miseries and demons and at the same time also attempting to conquer the advancing culture of reason. Voltaire was holding forth only a few years before the birth of Joseph's parents. Both Emerson and Thoreau were writing at the same time as Joseph. Threatened by a possible turning away from magic and belief, evangelical fundamentalism was a strong force in Joseph's childhood.

Great numbers of people sought a myth of reward to counterbalance the hardships and miseries of real life. The Bible needed support. There could be nothing better than a second witness to the miracles. It was in this context that the Book of Mormon was thought to bring new proof.

Clearly, however, the one thing for which Joseph did not prepare was the development and importance of science and analytical reasoning.

Further, the Enlightenment argued against authoritarianism and in favor of individual freedom. Such a new influence was frightening to many people. Joseph spoke for authoritarianism and sought to erase the separation of church and state.

Such a move may have been popular with those he sought to reach, but in terms of the history of ideas, it was exactly the wrong move. An attempt to block the force of history may be comforting for the moment, but the force of history cannot be blocked.

It may be suggested the Book of Mormon can be seen as an exercise in "splitting" and "reversal (Ibid, p. 223)." Splitting is the defense mechanism that seeks to divide the world into black and white (good and bad--God and Satan) instead of approaching it in its true gray condition. Reversal is when the characters trade places. The good become bad, the strong become weak, &c.

Anderson (1999) felt Joseph's childhood dynamic could be summarized as follows:

On a psychological level, he oscillated between the deprivation of an unstable childhood and the psychological trauma of his surgery. Consequently, he regressed, drawing on the magic and omnipotent defenses of a very early child-hood to resolve the later Oedipal fears and being locked in at a childhood stage characterized by magic, fantasy, splitting, omnipotence, devaluation, projection, and denial. In my view this earlier emotional age was a fixation point that he had only tenuously left before. Later in life, I believe he applied this omnipotent privilege and counter-phobic defense to his sexual life, at this point he most closely fit the unofficial sub-classification of "phallic narcissist," whose prototype in the Book of Mormon was Ammon. These attempts, in my opinion, account for the Book of Mormon's compensating and conquering fantasies of invincibility and conquest by the sword. They also suggest the rather gloomy prognosis that he would never escape from extreme fantasy compensation for his real life (Anderson, p. 224).

Thus, in compensating for exploitation and shame, Joseph turned the tables in his account and displayed his need for adoration. Because of his intense envy of others as well as his expectation others were seeking to exploit him (as he was seeking to exploit them) Joseph developed a profound lack of trust. All of this was masked by the appearance of his powerful wonderfulness. These are also diagnostic elements of narcissism (see Kernberg (1975) and especially Kohut (1984).

A defining element of narcissism is a marked lack of empathy. It appears Joseph's childhood experiences were either praise, at the hands of his mother and family, or scorn, at the hands of those he sought to swindle. Joseph appears to have developed, instead, a believable response of sympa-

269

thy when it suited his purposes. It stands to reason, therefore, there is little place for empathy in the writings of Joseph. He was interested in achievement (in the service of the ideal self) rather than empathic opening.

In order for Joseph to establish his worldview and construction as central, he had to devalue other world views and constructions. According to Anderson's (1999) account, the device of splitting may be seen in the First Book Of Nephi. There, Anderson held, Nephi, who is the son of Lehi, sees the established and influential Catholic Church as a kind of "evil empire."

> I saw among the notions of the Gentiles, the foundation of a great church...which is most abominable above all other churches, which slayeth the Saints of God...and I saw the devil, that he was the founder of it. And I also saw gold, and silver, and silks, and scarlets, and fine twined linen, and all manner of precious clothing; and I saw many harlots...and also for the

praise of the world do they destroy the Saints of God, and also bring them down into captivity (1 Nephi: 13:4-9).

According to this account, the Mormon Church is considered to be good, whereas the Catholic Church is considered to be bad. Good and bad are split apart.

And [the angel] saith unto me, Look...Behold, there is save it be, two churches: the one is the church of the Devil; wherefore, whoso belongeth not to the church of the Lamb of God, belongeth to that great church, which is the mother of abominations; and she is the whore of all the earth (1 Nephi: 14:10).

Thus the world was seen in polarized terms.

Also at this time (as a young man) Joseph was moving steadily away from magic and into Christianity. This, however, appears to be a shift in focus, not in procedure. The conquering of reality by (higher) fantasy continues to be the method. It is important that while Isaac Hale, father of Joseph's wife Emma, constantly pressured Joseph toward conventional living, Joseph's parents constantly pressured him toward the supernatural.

A popular book in Joseph's environment at the time was The Lost Ten Tribes by Ethan Smith. It was certainly not out of character for Joseph take it upon himself to also "solve" the riddle of the tribes proposed in the book with the story of his strange ocean-going boats.

Joseph's need to be special required him to develop a sense of competition. He needed to be the hero. It is interesting that Joseph had a vision that told him only he could receive revelations (Brodie, p. 92). He also devised a Deity that tended to operate in black and white. It is interesting that even Joseph's notion of heaven was competitive.

In a word, the Book of Mormon is a chronicle of conquering, enduring, and prevailing (us-them).

The good guys, who opt to follow the revealed "truths", are saved. The bad guys, who turn away, are not. Following to the prophet's word is essential.

After the appearance of the Book of Mormon, Joseph took up leading his religion. He naturally drew people to him due to his charisma as well as his (to these people) appearance as an amazing authority. He appeared as he desired to be: invincible.

Projective Identification is the device behind charisma. Here, one's desire to be special is projected into followers who then feel special in one's presence. Joseph was so adept at this he could actually make others see visions (Brodie, p. 74). Joseph was also adept at generating up devotion; his converts actually gave over their property. They were part of the special group, those "ordained of God."

Joseph took his flock west to Ohio, Missouri, and Illinois before they made the long and perilous trek to Utah. He was able to make himself unwelcome in each place. The faithful frequently talk about how the Mormons were persecuted, but Joseph played a large part in setting this up.

Fundamentally Joseph's religion was at odds with the American spirit of the times, especially on the frontier. According to Russell (2010) the development of American culture had been a tension against the Puritan forces of Godliness, Piety, and responsibility (Jonathan Edwards) as opposed to the urges of personal enjoyment and pleasure. American democracy was, in an important way, the enemy of freedom and pleasure. Simply put American "freedom" of the time was burdensome and restrictive (p. 47). Life on the frontier was more open.

Joseph's autocracy would not have gelled well with those on the frontier. Further, he had little interest in belonging. He was primarily interested in his own ends.

As a rule, frontier people had little use for the responsibilities of citizenship. Friction with the Mormons was all but inevitable.

Cannon and Knapp (1913) argued:

And here we touch the reason why
Mormonism, with all its elements of
attractiveness, roused furious and
unreasoning opposition wherever it
came in contact with non-Mormon
communities. It sought to establish
not only a church but a government,
and a government whose character
was opposed to every instinct and
tradition of American life. The pioneer of the Mississippi valley saw
no reason why Joseph Smith might
not talk with angels; and the idea of
a scripture showing God's working
on the Western Hemisphere appealed to his continental pride. But
when asked to renounce his liberty
of action, and when told that he
must yield implicit obedience to the
decrees of an irresponsible ruler, the
pioneer rebelled; and he denounced
those who did not reel as traitors to
the principles of American life. The
democracy of the land was rough
and chaotic; but it was deep and vital and it revolted instinctively at

the idea of a theocratic despotism.
(p. 27).

Actually, Joseph's drive to be superior impelled him to take over the supervision of both the spiritual as well as the temporal affairs of his followers. As well as a religion, he was establishing a social order. Brodie (1945) remarked that unlike Jesus, Joseph's kingdom was primarily of this world. In Mormonism the priesthood was available to everyone (who was male).

Further, Joseph's kingdom allowed no criticism. He was not at all adept at compromise. It was his way or not (splitting). Joseph set up the town of Nauvoo, Illinois on his own laws. He then petitioned the U.S. Congress to set Nauvoo aside from the United States, as its own "independent Federal territory (Brodie, p. 356). Nauvoo was to be the Kingdom of God on Earth with no interference by external laws.

And Joseph, of course, was the king of the Kingdom of God.

At the same time, Joseph knew his people couldn't really survive if they left the United States. Yet compromise was not thinkable. His solution was to go west to the still primitive, undeveloped wilderness.

Joseph, who was charming--especially when things went his way--was always taken with the ladies (Anderson, p. 297). It was perhaps inevitable his thoughts began to include polygamy. Aside from Joseph's healthy libido, there are at least two major impulses behind this. The first is that his marriage to Emma was essentially the marriage of an ideal self to a woman who responded to it. This was sort of a "wonderful arrangement," not the love of two flawed human beings with genuine empathic resonance for each other. Consequently the marital troubles between these two would have centered around the need to maintain that idealization.

The second was Joseph's need to be in control rather than bowing to any other convention. With the event of polygamy among the Mormons, only Mormon marriages really counted. The marriages of others did not. This was, in essence, a short form of the notion that reality was essentially what Joseph said it was.

Nonetheless, polygamy was never officially admitted by the Mormons, as it would certainly have called down the wrath of the federal and state governments--thus adding even more opposition to the burden of the Mormons.

Essentially it was Joseph's megalomania that drove him too far.

> He [Joseph] was not only candidate for President, but also mayor of Nauvoo, judge of the municipal court, merchant of the leading store, hotel-keeper, official temple architect, real-estate agent, contractor, recorder of deeds, steam -boat-owner, trustee-in-trust for all the finances of his church, lieutenant-general of the Nauvoo Legion, spiritual adviser and Lord's communicant to the true church, King of the new Kingdom of God, and husband

of almost fifty wives (Brodie, p. 366).

The pivotal issue was polygamy. Joseph had gotten into a land dispute with a man named William Law, a wealthy Canadian convert to the Mormons. As the dispute heated, Law bought a printing press and sued Joseph. He printed only one edition of his paper, but that edition exposed Joseph's involvement not only in shady land deals but also in polygamy. This information threatened Joseph's image as infallible and divinely guided.

Terrified--we must imagine--Joseph, who it appears could only think in terms of suppression at that time, called the city counsel together.

> The city counsel now declared that the press was libelous and must be destroyed. Joseph issued a proclamation declaring it a civic nuisance; a portion of the Legion marched to the office, wrecked the press, pied the type, and burned every issue of

the hated paper that could be found
(Ibid. p. 377).

This was a federal crime.

Even at this point, Joseph could have saved himself by simply telling the truth. But his psychological adjustment couldn't tolerate this. Telling the
truth would amount to abandoning the invincible
ideal self and identifying with the real self. This
act, which would have been humiliating for another, was not psychologically possible for Joseph.
The conflict broke him.

He simply did not know what to do. First he
went across the Mississippi in a great storm, but
then was persuaded by his brother Hyrum to return
to Nauvoo where he was arrested and taken to jail
in Carthage. It was in the jail at Carthage that
Joseph and Hyrum were assassinated by a mob.

Joseph's martyrdom elevated his stature among
the Mormons and was the impetus for the beginning of the trek west.

The exposure of polygamy shattered Joseph's fantasy of his ideal self. He had always been able to hold reality at bay before. His mother had visions, and in Joseph's childhood home dreams and visions were routinely conflated as well as there being confusion about dreams and reality. There had been little reality testing in the family.

But Joseph's task in life was not reality testing, it was the development of an omnipotent fantasy.

Even before Joseph's family moved to New York, his mother "knew" Joseph would be a prophet. His father thought he was the family genius and also that he would be a prophet. Clearly, being a prophet was the greatest thing one could be. All his life Joseph desperately needed to be "the great one," and his followers needed him to be that as well.

They found each other. Both needed to rise above the mere grind of reality and attain "perfection," and the "blissful state" of lost Eden. Anderson (1999) suggested Joseph was able to touch "the heart of every person who has felt small, helpless, and alone (p. 242)."

Surely Joseph possessed a remarkable imagination.

The power vacuum created following Joseph's death was filled by his loyal companion Brigham Young. It was Young that began the migration to Utah.

Far more tyrannical and dogmatic than Joseph, Brigham was similarly uneducated. He attended school for eleven days in his lifetime. What he lacked in imagination and natural charm, however, Brigham made up for in his superior organizational skills. The journey across the plains was perilous and often brutal. Scores of people died. Rarely has such a price been paid to escape the evils of the United States.

In Brigham's hand the Mormons became a rigidly maintained social order in addition to being a religion.

Brigham was extremely black and white in his views. One was "with us" or "against us."

In the 1830's, Mormonism, a mixture of superstition and tradition, appealed, as Saints themselves admitted, to the fearful, the credulous, and the downtrodden...Then as now the Mormons viewed life—and history--as an endless struggle with the devil. "There are only two churches on the earth," Young explained, "only two parties. God leads the one, the Devil the other (Ibid, p. 16-17).

For example, Young found it quite reasonable to steal from the "gentiles" (non LDS people) (Hirshson, p. 63). In his view violence and holy war was to be raged against the gentiles. In fact, Brigham fiercely believed that the kingdom of God was the only legitimate government. He, of course, was its chief representative on Earth.

Cannon and Knapp (1913) pointed out:

But deep down in his heart, Brigham Young remained a New

England Puritan to the day of his death. His was the Puritan's domineering temper, the Puritan's self-righteousness, the Puritan's impatience with other people's sins; and his, likewise, the Puritan's abiding faith in the virtue of work, the advantage of thrift, and the necessity of keeping on the good side of a testy-tempered Providence (p. 146-47).

Brigham held that God demanded "universal obedience" (Hirshson, p. 92-3). To Brigham "freedom" and "democracy" were meaningless words. He sought isolation in order to avoid outside influence. Clearly, he held, LDS law superseded US law. He believed that the United States was destined to collapse, and Mormonism would take over. He went so far as to swear "everlasting enmity" to the United States. Further, Brigham assumed every loyal member of his group thought just like him.

Even more misogynistic than Joseph, Brigham held that women were stupid and had to be led.

Further, it was their duty to submit cheerfully. Travelers to Salt Lake City remarked that the women looked overworked and troubled (Ibid, p. 133). Essentially rural polygamy appeared as a state of slavery.

It may be said Joseph created the religion, and Brigham molded it into a functioning autocracy. There were essentially no free elections in Utah. People voted the way Brigham wanted them to vote. To do so was pleasing to God. There was no (voiced) disagreement.

> He had two purposes in life; two purposes so fused together that his un-analytic mind doubtless thought them one. He would build the Mormon colony into a strong, self-supporting, self-sufficing church-state; and he would keep that state absolutely subject to his rule (Cannon and Knapp, p. 179).

As might be expected large numbers of Mormons were from the lower classes and were uneducated. Many were from the oppressed classes of Europe. Essentially they knew what Brigham wanted them to know. Anxiety prevailed. Either one obeyed or one died.

This situation, it seems, was literally played out at the Mountain Meadows Massacre, the darkest hour in Utah history. An entire wagon train was wiped out, men, women, and children (Brooks, 1950). Such was the xenophobic atmosphere among the Mormons at the time.

Brigham would also brook no interference from the federal government and made life difficult if not impossible for officials such as federal judges, commissioners, &c. The hostility coming from Salt Lake City toward the U.S. government was a major issue in congress at the time and resulted in a contingent of the U.S. Army being sent to Utah to deal with the "rebellion."

Cannon and Knapp (1913) claimed Brigham never came in contact with the real life of the nation, save to defy it, flout it, and do his best to change it (p. 9).

He matched his wits against the might of the United States government, and did not come off second-best. He yielded in outward seeming to federal power; but in reality he was emperor of his little realm to the hour of his death, and his subjects never doubted his supremacy. He drove federal appointees in disgrace from his kingdom, and took their positions for himself and his favorites. No matter how overwhelming the power with which he was dealing, Brigham Young never was a suppliant. He stormed, bullied, lied, intrigued, finessed, cajoled; he never pleaded for mercy nor owned himself in need of mercy. He met chastisement with fresh provocation (p. 10).

Brigham tolerated no opposition. There were a reported 177 murders reported during this time of people who had been deemed undesirable (Hirshson, p. 175).

Murders were committed in the Mormon kingdom, not to defy Brigham's authority, but to maintain it. In many cases, perhaps in most cases, he Brigham knew nothing of the deed until it was done. In many cases, perhaps in most cases, he regretted the over-violent acts of his followers. But those acts grew directly out of his own teachings and ambitions, and Brigham recognized this fact when he failed to punish or even to condemn the criminals who had served him too well (Ibid, p. 271).

According to Brigham, who had continued the practice of polygamy, only more openly--he is said to have had 55 wives--lectured that love was a "false sentiment." He favored arranged marriages. Apparently women and daughters had little say in this.

Primarily Brigham ran things his way. Seeing at times to be humorous in a folksy kind of way, there was very little religion in Brigham's speeches. Also his lack of schooling was apparent.

> The prophet's speeches, moreover, resembled those of no other clergyman. He usually ignored the Bible, filling his sermons instead with hints on stock raising and fence building, tales of Mormon sufferings, advice to the lovelorn, and anecdotes (Ibid, p. 244).

A reporter for the New York Herald wrote in 1858:

> He uses whatever word comes first to express his ideas, so his language is quite original and his expressions frequently very telling. His language does not flow along like a torrent, but is strong, harsh and commanding...He could not minister to a graceful and accomplished society, but he is a man preeminently quali-

fied to rule a mountain people with a rod of iron and a gloved hand...

Young's speech reflected his New England background and meager education. Possessing what Burton called "a mind uncorrupted by books," the prophet continually mispronounced "impetus." "Provincialisms of his Vermont boyhood and his Western manhood still cling to him... "he says 'leetle,' 'beyond' and 'disremember.' An irrepressible conflict between his nominatives and verbs now and then crop out in expressions like 'they was (Ibid.)'

Brigham turned away from education and believed in exorcism. "Young disliked education and feared educated men (Ibid.)" The University of Utah, for example, has been a pointedly secular school since its inception in 1851.

But education and new ideas were not all that was on Brigham's list of things to avoid. He disliked Jews, and considered Black people to be the

290

lowest. He was opposed to Lincoln, and flatly hated the United States. East Coast influence was feared. He was careful to have no contact with the outside world and detested non-Mormons. Brigham instigated a boycott of non Mormon businesses. He ran a rigid ship, and he was its undisputed captain.

What Brigham did not understand, he feared (Ibid, p. 323).

Brigham opposed alcohol largely as a rejection of influence from the outside world. But he knew that there were Saints who drank it. He therefore took up making whiskey, which he sold to the locals at inflated prices. Though he opposed its consumption, he saw no reason not to profit from its sale to sinners. Apparently, Brigham made the worst whiskey on record.

This neat autocracy was doomed by the coming of the transcontinental railroad, which ironically was completed in Utah. This meant outside influence could arrive quickly instead of by an arduous journey overland. Increasingly after this American born converts began to leave Salt Lake City. Foreign born converts, however, did not.

Brigham Young himself was eventually tried for polygamy and murder (Ibid, p. 305-307). But so corrupt had become the Mormon law, that he was exonerated.

Despite all this, Brigham's followers remained steadfastly loyal.

> To Mormons the exodus to Utah illustrates the determination of God's people to find a Promised Land in the face of Satanic opposition. Utah's prosperity shows God's consideration for His Saints and fulfills the promise of a better life for all believers. And the struggle against the Gentile symbolizes the Saints' determination to survive and live their religion. In this light Young's every move becomes as sacred to his people as Mohammed's is to Moslems and Buddha's to Buddhists (Ibid, p. 322).

The true picture of Brigham Young, however, was different. He was a mixture of good and bad. "He professed inspiration from Jesus but shunned the Master's fundamental teachings: love for one's enemies, meekness, and the abandonment of material things (Ibid.)"

> Young left to his followers a mixed legacy. He left a people determined to survive and prosper but one afraid of a monster called Satan and fearful of excommunication and damnation. Like Young, the Saints are a people of limited intellectual interests, a people more concerned with irrigation than with pure mathematics, a people, now as then, involved with their own history and no one else's...Young desired unquestioning obedience above all else, and made Utah the thinking man' graveyard. Where another self-proclaimed chosen people stressed education and looked for guidance to the rabbi, or teacher of the law, the Saints ridiculed the wise man (Ibid.)

In 1877 Brigham Young contracted cholera morbus and died. There was a massive funeral in Salt Lake City. The man, who stressed obedience over thinking, and in fact routinely ridiculed wise men, had forcefully prevailed until the end.

A period of some modernization and accommodation followed the death of Brigham Young. Polygamy essentially died with Brigham, and Utah was admitted to statehood. The animosity to the United States softened but not the Mormon penchant for power. Increasingly the "good" was associated with material prosperity, and big business became "thoroughly beatified." (Brodie, p. 402). Education was sought, but primarily as a means of attaining economic power.

As more and more outsiders moved into Salt Lake City, it slowly took on a more urbane texture. As this is written, in fact, approximately one third of the population of Salt Lake City is Mormon. The mayor of the city is non-Mormon. This, however, is in contrast to the more rural sections of the state, where Mormonism in more or less "traditional" form remains.

The Mormon-non-Mormon divide continues to this day. It was this I experienced as a child. Little did I know the context in which I lived. I thought I was just being a kid in the world. I had yet to discover that, as a rule, especially us-them, Mormons are loath to cross this divide with any degree of sincerity. Getting lost away from the Mormon base continues to be a big concern. More moderate Mormons often attempt to reconcile their religion and the popular culture.

Still, as a result of their historical legacy, Mormons tend to focus on Mormon issues and practices and, as a rule, do not pursue more urbane or worldly sensibilities. Rome is about as far away as ever. All that stuff beyond the boundaries of Mormonism remains the province of Satan.

Additionally, Mormon people tend to be highly invested in *appearing* Mormon--but not too much. It is important to look like you are a happy member of the larger group, though this is done in a sort of Happy Meal fashion. There are a myriad of signals and signs to separate in-groupers from out-groupers. These traverse the gamut from such things as drinking coffee and alcohol or smoking all the way to grooming standards (no long hair) and various idioms.

At the present time it may be said the LDS church has shifted in its approach from being what might be called iconoclastic, rigid-tending, xenophobic, and self-focused radicals to a group of squeaky-clean, obedient, and apparently social corporate types. Essentially, this transformation began in the 1960s during the era of hippies and anti View Nam War crusades--which were largely criticized by Mormon leaders. Bill Clinton is rumored to have said, "If you thought the sixties were a good thing, you are probably a Democrat; if you thought the sixties were a bad thing, you are probably a Republican."

The Mormons became entirely Republican. A musical called "Saturday's Warrior" debuted on the campus of the church owned Brigham Young University in 1973. At that time many Mormons were upset at the events of the sixties and felt the values of an earlier time were being lost. The heroes of the musical urge their wayward kin to return to the folds of the doctrine and its strict moral code along with clean-cut principles espoused by the church.

In other words, shun hippies and their ubiquitous popular culture and return to church—where you will be "saved."

At roughly this same time an LDS apostle named Harold B. Lee (who later became president of the church) took charge of a committee called "The All-Church Coordinating Committee (Bowman, 2012)." The committee's task was to coordinate the curricula of church programs. Lee went on to also centralize power and establish a review committee for all church publications. Manuscripts were reviewed for adherence to theological "correctness" as well as to the goals and values of the church.

When a manuscript is approved it is said in church lingo to be "correlated." Correlated works were opposed to the social upheavals of the 1960s and were sympathetic with earlier "progressive" views of the twentieth century. These earlier views stressed, among other things, order, moral virtue, industriousness, and a view that education, effective government, and committed volunteers could raise poor people and immigrants to be productive members of the American middle class.

Corporate thinking, among Mormon leaders came of age.

Interestingly, it was during the sixties that IBM Corporation was routinely a central target of counter-culture satire. IBM was the "them" to be overcome. Yet IBM wasn't the only corporation opposed to the free love moment. Corporate structure in general by-passed the sixties and continued its earlier established working methodology, power organization, and attitudes.

Harold B. Lee was greatly impressed by great corporate leaders who turned to politics, such as Nelson Rockefeller and George Romney.

> ...Lee, and the mid-century Mormon leaders who aided him, were deeply influenced by the brisk pragmatism of these men, and so correlation remade Mormonism in the image of the data-driven American corporation, governed by committees, based on consensus, and institutionally conservative (Bowman, 2012).

Thus, in the name of corporate efficiency, individual insights were urged to be reduced to officially approved manuals. An article in the LDS Church News, an official organ of the Mormon church, put it this way:

> As Church members, we are asked to prayerfully prepare Church lessons and activities. We are to seek personal revelation from the Lord and study Church materials and instructions. We can counsel with our presidencies or committees and seek advice from priesthood leaders as we strive to meet the needs of those we serve. The scriptures are an invaluable resource. But we may be tempted to do more, to turn to unofficial lesson plans, resources and information found in books and on the Internet. But leaders and teachers in the Church do themselves and the people they serve a disservice when they turn to unofficial —not correlated —

materials in the planning of lessons and activities. Correlation is an inspired effort overseen by the First Presidency and the Quorum of the Twelve to simplify the programs of the Church and unify Latter-day Saints in faith and doctrine. Since the early 1960s, Church members have seen the results of more than four decades of correlation efforts, established to: Maintain purity of doctrine.Emphasize the importance of the family and the home. Place all the work of the Church under priesthood direction. Establish proper relationships among the organizations of the Church. Achieve unity and order in theChurch. Ensure simplicity of programs and materials (see LDS).

A clear implication is that individual thinking is no only not necessary but is a *disservice* to the church. Church leaders praised this program as it brings everything into line. Do what you are told. And only what you are told.

...Saturday's Warriors...characters
love their family, strive to do what
is right, and demonstrate a relent-
lessly chipper confidence that right
living will bring happiness. They
are morally upstanding—and almost
uniformly bland, not to mention
fearful of the world outside their
faith (Bowman).

Inevitably, however, this isolationism proved to
be little asset in the context of the plurality of
evolving present day America. More revisions
were necessary.

Recently a campaign called "I'm a Mormon" has
tried to foster such a pluralist image. Even Mormon missionaries are now instructed not to (directly) "counter" other faiths but seek to "add to
them"—at least initially before talk of conversion
in entertained. Mormons are urged to reach out to
their neighbors and find worth in the world beyond the borders of Mormonism.

This Mormonism, the Mormonism of David Archuleta and Stephanie Meyer, is defined less by rigorous conformity and personal self-discipline than by the ability to project a wholesome pluralism—to reflect back to present America the things which it values most, albeit edited to a PG rating (Ibid).

The result is a weird, somewhat stiff cartoon that tends to amplify its surface-only nature. Yet like a new fender on an old car, the paint doesn't quite match. It's a modern fender all right, but the same traditional doctrine is waiting just beneath.

A major reason for this is the "I am a Mormon" campaign has itself been correlated. The campaign only displays "proper" Mormons, those who clearly display what the campaign is attempting to portray. "See, we are just like you." Only we are not. We have been specially selected. Also we are *in* the world but not *of* the world. Behind our congenial image, we are only saying what our manual allows (see irresistibledisgrace).

Pareene (2012) suggested modern day Mormonism owes a great deal to Walt Disney and wondered at the practice of (literally) taking communion with Wonder Bread.

> ...[This] Mormonism is the impossibly cheery "Donny and Marie" variety, not the armed apocalyptic homesteading cult member variety. Tolstoy — referring to the scrappy/crazy 19th century version — called Mormonism "the American religion," and he decidedly did not mean that as a compliment. But the modern church still deserves the title. It's the Coca-Cola religion, with a brand that denotes a sort of upbeat corporate Americanness, considered cheesy by elites but undeniably popular in pockets of the heartland and abroad.

In addition to these trends, the lack of separation between the Mormon leadership and the Utah legislature continues largely due to a policy of equal representation among counties. Thus, each county has an equal number of representatives in the legislature. This effectively minimizes the influence of Salt Lake City, where approximately half the state's population resides--and who are significantly more egalitarian.

For example the Utah legislature continues the practice of opposing the drinking of alcohol on one hand, but on the other rakes in a giant profit from its sale due to exorbitant mark-ups.

And, to this day, there are a significant number of people in Utah whose center and entire personal experience is within Mormonism. These are people who tend to have little grasp of the "outside" world, its richness, its diversity, its culture, and its rhythms. To these people, everything is seen in terms of what they know: through the lens of Mormonism.

These were my neighbors in my childhood.

Still the trend is toward further integration of the Mormon people with the world. Due to the widely expanding access to media and global input, outside views are increasingly available. Of course the messages from the pulpit continue as well. These warn about external influence, and urge followers to be faithful to (correlated) Mormon principles to the exclusion of other sources.

PART III

Since the start, Mormons have bristled at critcism. This includes even minor criticism or failure to take the position seriously. Arguing with Mormons is often futile (especially us-them Mormons). Routinely they don't stick to logic, and it is uncommon to come across someone with any kind of expanded or urbane knowledge base.

Further, as argued earlier, one is not seen as disagreeing with a position so much as assailing a defense. If the goal of Mormonism is to maintain a commitment to and identification with an idealistic position on the part of "believers," options opposed to this must be neutralized. Anything from polite explanation to intimidation and rage may be used to deter such input.

Actually, a fair amount of the time Mormons run on "beliefs." And these are often held to be more important than facts. Much Mormon argument is designed to assure in-groupers they have nothing to fear.

A good example is the following. In a review of Joseph Smith: The Making of a Prophet (Vogel, 2004) Walker (2006) said:

> However, in borrowing from Anderson and Morain, who utilized an approach termed "applied psychoanalysis," Vogel adheres to a modality that requires a significant amount of elaboration and assumptions. Although psychoanalysis is grounded in scientific and academic history, it is only loosely based on the body of knowledge about social and psychological phenomena, and when utilized in evaluating limited historical information it requires extensive speculation (p. 1).

So much for psychoanalysis--or anything of significance it may have discovered. (Actually, contrary to the above author's views, psychoanalytic and psychodynamic approaches are alive and well and deliver empirically demonstrable results [see Goodheart, Kazdon, and Sternberg, 2006; Levy, Ablon, and Kachele, 2012.]. The author, apparently not having studied psychoanalysis in any depth, nevertheless finds it is safe to assail it with ease in the service of making Mormon orthodoxy appear solid.

It is this practice of dismissing with great energy what one does not understand or is external to one's knowledge base that is common.

Another common approach is to dismiss any view that gets any fact wrong. One wrong fact negates the entire effort.

Actually Mormons I have known tend to conflate knowing and believing anyway, using them interchangeably in grammar designed for expressions of knowing. In "Testimony Meetings" individuals stand and assure the congregation, "I *know* the Gospel is true." This is meant to be reassuring to everyone. But it really says little.

Wittgenstein (1969) argued:

13. "There is a hand there" follows from the proposition "He knows that there's a hand there". But from his utterance "I know..." it does not follow that he does know it.

14. That he does know takes some shewing.

15. It needs to be *shewn* that no mistake was possible. Giving the assurance "I know" doesn't suffice. For it is after all only an assurance that I can't be making a mistake, and it needs to be *objectively* established that I am not making a mistake about *that*.

16. "If I know something, then I also know that I know it, etc." amounts to: "I know that" means "I

am incapable of being wrong about that". But whether I am so needs to be established objectively.

"Knowing" in the Mormon usage thus urges an assent to the speaker who is presumed to have a special kind of knowing not requiring any support.

Clearly, Mormonism developed before the significant advance of academic analysis and wide-ranging public efforts at education in the United States. Joseph's prophesies are no match for the techniques of science with its ever more sophisticated abilities at measurement and analytical research. They are also no match for linguistic analysis and its focus on the logic of grammar.

There has been no archeological evidence to support Joseph's stories. His "translations" have been shown to be bogus. He was sadly taken in by two ordinary mummies sold to him, and his "translations" of the Book of Abraham were fake (Brodie, p. 175). Legions have been amused that Joseph found the plates to a revolutionary world religion in a hill located right behind his house.

Joseph's work was focused for a group who knew nothing of all that. They were searching for answers, not long careers as students in academic institutions. They simply did not demand the level of ancillary support. They, rather, accepted supernatural explanations as well as the power of magic. They were not disciplined users of the language, and they were most certainly not students of the logic of grammar. They, consequently, thought words could mean anything they wanted them to or even that individual meanings were the case. Wittgenstein (1956) would have terrified them.

If Joseph's ideas were no match for science or recent advances in linguistic analysis, these ideas were definitely not ready for the development of postmodernism.

When knowledge and truth are "de-centered," there is no longer one truth. Truth becomes a function of perspective, use, and contextual application. When the goal becomes to examine and learn to see from as many perspectives as possible, the rigid maintaining of one view is seen to be of little value.

Further, in such a context, power is seen as anathema. The welcoming and inclusion of diversity, on the other hand, becomes the sought after goal. This is especially true for colonial power of the type sought by Mormons to preserve themselves and render others into a state of subordination.

Akin to this has been the devaluing of alterity, which is precisely the logic used by the Mormon founders. In the creation of alterity there are three steps. First, a distinction is made between us and the others--who are not seen as individuals. Secondly, unwanted or devalued elements in the self are split off and then projected onto the "others" (I am good; you are bad). The third step is to institutionalize this arrangement.

Essentially this is utilized as a division between Mormons and non-Mormons, but the Mormons have also energized this process when faced with major new ideas that were not of their own devising. For example, Mormons strongly opposed attempts to cut down on the practice of racism. Only recently (1978) have they allowed Black persons to enter the LDS priesthood. The Mormons were very energetic in their opposition to the

Equal Rights Amendment, which was nothing more than a statement of equal standing for persons of all genders.

More recently it has been proposed the racism of the church was attributable to Brigham Young. It seems he was "influenced by the common beliefs of the time." No mention was made of the references in the Book of Mormon that held black skin was a punishment for negative behavior (Stack, 2013).

Bushman (see Stack) said, "Mormons believe that their leaders are in regular communication with God, so if you say Young could make a serious error, he says, it brings into question all of the prophet's inspiration.

Nonetheless:

And, to be perfectly frank, there have been times when members or leaders in the church have simply made mistakes. There may have been things said or done that were

312

not in harmony with our values, principles or doctrine," Dieter F. Uchtdorf, second counselor in the faith's governing First Presidency, said in October's LDS General Conference. "I suppose the church would be perfect only if it were run by perfect beings. God is perfect, and his doctrine is pure. But he works though us—his imperfect children—and imperfect people make mistakes (Ibid.)."

Yet the message and the insight seems to stop at this particular place. If mistakes were made about Black people, is it not possible (even likely) mistakes have also been made about women, gay people, transexuals? How long will it take for these mistakes to be realized?

Mormons long exerted unusual energy, time, and wealth in an attempt to prevent the acceptance of gay marriage. It might be noted such a movement originated outside Mormonism.

The stand against gay marriage has, itself, created numerous tragedies (see O'Donnovan, 1994, 2004.).

One may or may not hear empathy expressed for the humanity of such groups. It sometimes has sounded almost as if Black people, women, and gay people are not human in the same way correctly obedient Mormon people are. They are simply other.

Recently the Mormon Church did appear to have a change of heart on the gay marriage issue. After their vigorous stand against such unions, the Mormons ostensibly stopped opposing this issue in public. Though there has been no doctrinal change, the cessation of their very vocal opposition to gay marriage withdrew one of the largest obstacles against such unions.

When a Federal Judge finally ruled Utah's opposition to gay marriage was unconstitutional--due to the considerable efforts of attorney Peggy Tomsic and her colleagues--the state as well as the Mormon church was quick to denounce the action and plea for a stay of enforcement.

Utah Gov. Gary Herbert released a statement that said he was "very disappointed an activist federal judge is attempting to override the will of the people of Utah" and said he would work with Acting Attorney General Brian L. Tarbet "to determine the best course to defend traditional marriage within the borders of Utah (Adams, 2013)."

The LDS church was quick to issue similar comments supporting "traditional marriage" within the state of Utah.

Both of these sets of comments pointedly elided the fact the "will of the people of Utah" and Utah's definition of "traditional marriage" (alone) had just been declared unconstitutional. This seems to underline the loose connection many in Utah have with the United States entire. A letter to the Salt Lake Tribune entitled "Tell Judge To Take A Hike" suggested the governor and Legislature to tell Federal Judge Selby "to take a hike and stay out of our business." After all: "Utah decided in the proper manner that we would not allow gay marriages in our state, so that is the law. And no one can tell us it's not (Green, 2013)."

Never mind the fact the law was passed several years before when sixty four percent of Utah citizens supported it. Today that percentage has apparently dropped to twenty nine. The state, nevertheless, appealed the ruling to the United States Supreme Court. Holding out to the end, Utah argued only the state should be able to decide these matters, no one else (i.e., who is different).

Even after the U.S. Supreme Court issued a stay to the implementation of the law while it was under appeal, Governor Herbert went so far as to declare the State of Utah would not honor the same sex marriages that had been legally performed in the state. President Obama and U.S. Attorney General Holder then countered that such marriages would be seen as legal in the eyes of the Federal Government.

Additionally, it may be seen Mormons are significantly involved with revisionist history. It is as if Joseph's drive for perfection continues apace.

Updates to both the history and the doctrine appear consistently.

In addition to the timely revelation including Black males in the priesthood (and the attempt to play down all the terrible claims previously laid against them), elisions and uncomfortable accounts often simply disappear.

Another wonderful example is the following:

> Martin Harris was questioned by a Palmyra lawyer, who asked him pointedly: "Did you see the plates and the engravings upon them with your bodily eyes?" To which he replied: "I did not see them as I do that pencil-case, yet I saw them with the eye of faith; I saw them just as distinctly as I see anything around me--though at the time they were covered with a cloth (Brodie, p. 78).

Since a central teaching of the Mormons is that their place in heaven will be determined by their ability to follow the proper teachings, other views are routinely thought of as needing helpful correction. This will make a wholesale welcome of diversity and inclusion difficult.

It may be argued that the focus of Mormonism is on obedience. This has been stressed throughout Mormon history far more than has empathy or the experience of the sacred. One does not resonate; one complies.

Further, resonance is not necessary even with God (Christian or otherwise). Obedience is.

How different the teachings of St. John of the Cross are from the those of Joseph Smith, and especially those of Brigham Young. It is amazing St. John was writing almost two hundred years before Joseph Smith:

THE ASCENT OF MOUNT CARMEL

Song of the soul that rejoices at that
high state of perfection which is the
union with God by the road of
spiritual negation.

Upon a dark, still night
When restless love burst flaming in my breast,
Oh happy chance, my flight—
I went unseen, unguessed,
While all my house lay quietly at rest.

Secure, with gloom above,
Up secret stairs disguised I made my way,
Oh happy chance, my love—
In gloom and his away
While at its rest my house in quiet lay

I went that happy night
In secret, guarded safe from all discerning,
And nothing was in sight—
No guide, no light for turning
Save that which in my heart of hearts was
 burning.

That light led clear before me
More certain than the brightest noonday sun
To where he waited for me,
The one I knew, the one:
He waited where there was no other, none.

Oh night that led and guided,
Oh night more lovely that the break of dawn;
Oh night, thou that united
The lover with his loved one,
Transformed her into his and lingered on!

Deep in my breast's white flower
Which I had kept untouched for him alone
He slept away the hour
And I caressed my own
While breezes made the cedars softly moan.

Upon the wall winds drifted
And while I drew my fingers through his hair,
His quiet hand he lifted
And struck my throat, and there
My senses were suspended unaware.

I lingered past recall
And laid my face upon my lover's hair;
I left myself, left all,
Abandoning my care,
Forgotten in the lilies white and fair.

--St. John of the Cross
Translated by Hugh Hagius

This clearly is a markedly different sensibility than that urged by Joseph Smith and Brigham Young. Here God is loving, a lover, with whom one seeks to fuse. Such fusion is directly through love and not through obedience. In fact St. John said: "In the evening of life, we will be judged on love alone (St. John, 1979)."

As any psychologist knows it is not love that takes one's voice away. It is dysfunction and abuse. It is impossible to abuse someone if he or she is genuinely granted a voice.

Alice Miller (1983) listed the conditions for such abuse.

> 1. The parents are the masters of the dependent child.
>
> 2. They determine in godlike fashion what is right and what is wrong.
>
> 3. The child is held responsible for the parents' anger.

4. The parents must always be shielded.

5. The child's life-affirming feelings pose a threat to the autocratic adult.

6. The child's will must be "broken" as soon as possible. All this must happen at a very early age so that the child "won't notice" and will therefore not be able to expose the adult.

These were very similar to the conditions Joseph imposed upon his followers in order to keep them focused on supporting his ideal vision of his kingdom and himself instead of the real world and his real self. Only the ideal self and its constructions were allowed. It is to be noticed these were also the requirements of Joseph's Deity. Though these principles are couched in loving talk about guidance and help, anything approved is okay. Everything else is bad and is to be corrected or shunned.

This distinction, further, was even more explicit with Brigham Young (Hirshson, p. 156).

Eliad (1957) pointed to the Greek distinction between the sacred and the profane. Profane space is of the world. Sacred space is of the divine.

This can be illustrated by noting the difference between sacred and profane time. Profane time is linear. It begins at one point and goes forward from there. It does not go back. It is the kind of time we think about in our daily lives. Sacred time, on the other hand, is static. When one moves from profane to sacred space, the sacred is always in the same space and the same time. It is always there, right where it was.

The argument is that the Christians simply cut off the sacred and emphasized the profane. Thus they made a big deal of their relics, documents, and historical truths. Eternal life had to be hooked onto the end of this one, as there was no other place for it.

Seen in this light it may be said that St. John's religion involved a direct experience of the sacred. Joseph's religion played out in obedience to the correct form of the profane.

However, it has been frequently argued (e.g. Campbell, 1988; Zimmer, 1948; et.al) that human life would be considerably poorer if all we had was (more or less factual) history. In such a case we would know a bit about what happened, but we would have no chronicle of the human heart--what life meant to people.

The meaning part becomes possible with the development of metaphor. And the big mistake in dealing with metaphors is to read them as factual statements. Then the evocative element collapses.

It is clear many early religious texts continue to suffer this fate, especially at the hands of fundamentalist interpreters. Here, the letter is often taken to be the law.

Neither Joseph Smith, Brigham Young, nor Mormons in general tend to metaphor. St. John might be said to have *bathed* in it. Thus in Mormonism a direct experience of the sacred does not tend to be a focal point.

For spiritualism Young substituted iron rule, priestly bondage, and materialism.   Far more than Joseph Smith, often ridiculed as money mad, he stressed the attainment of wealth as the greatest manifestation of God's favor (Hirshson, p. 297).

It must be stressed, however, I have met several Mormon people who do not fit the strict descriptions outlined above. These people have been far more urbane, educated, well traveled, and very much "of the world" as well as "in" it. They have, as a rule, been empathic, accepting, and tuned into an "outside view" as much as an "inside view" of the religion. They are clearly inclusive people instead of being us-them people.

In short, these have been remarkable people and are certainly a bright hope for the future.

But, to be fair, a direct experience of the sacred does not require a religious structure. It does not require being someone one is not (a good kid, instead of a real self). It does not require obedience, approval, or belonging. It does not require including or excluding, nor does it require relegating to lesser status the magnitude of suffering of people, human as oneself, simply because of chance of circumstance or what they happen to believe.

It is vital that the world overcome autocracy and rejection. Each heart matters and needs help. Each self must find out how to be itself in a developed way, because that is its contribution to human history. The truth is this genuine experience-- being exactly who one is. It is not to follow a preordained path decided by a parent or ecclesiastical figure.

It is the darkened eyes of Tarwater as he staggers from the burning woods toward the town below with his message. It is to move beyond a pathologically based isolationism or misleading cover-up in the service of protecting a narcissistic construction--which can be used as a club for those developing hearts who are categorized as being of the Devil.

REFERENCES

Anderson, R.D. Inside the Mind of Joseph Smith: Psychobiography and the Book of Mormon. Signature. 1999.

Arrington, L.J. Brigham Young: American Moses. Knopf. 1985.

Austin, J.L. "Truth." In J.L. Austin: Philosophical Papers. Ed. J.O. Urmson and G.J. Warnock. Oxford. 1961.

Bowman, M. "Mormon correlation: the bureaucratic reform policy that redefined Mormon culture." Slate. 04-25-2012.

Brodie, F.M. No Man Knows My History: The Life of Joseph Smith The Mormon Prophet. 2nd. Ed. Knopf. 1945/1971.

Brooks, J. The Mountain Meadow Massacre. U. Oklahoma. 1950/1970.

Campbell, J. Out in Inner Space: Metaphor as Myth and as Religion. Harper. 1986.

Campbell, J. Transformations of Myth Through Time. Harper. 1990.

Cannon, F.J. and Knapp, G.L. Brigham Young and his Mormon Empire. Revell. 1913.

Eliade, M. The Sacred and the Profane: The Significance of Religious Myth, Symbolism, and Ritual Within Life and Culture. Harcourt. 1957/1959.

Goodheart, C.D., Kazdin, A.E., and Sternberg, R.J. (Eds). Evidence-Based Psychotherapy: Where Practice and Research Meet. APA., 2006.

Gorrell, M. "Keeping the Faith When Talking With Lawmakers." Salt Lake Tribune. 08-15-2011. p. B3.

Harris, M.L. "Why is LDS Church Denying Past Doctrine?" Salt Lake Tribune, 03-11-12. p O4.

Hirshson, S. P. The Lion of the Lord: A Biography of Brigham Young. Knopf. 1969.

Irresistibledisgrace. http://irresistibledisgrace.-wordpress.com/2012/04/03/the-i-am-a-mormon-campaign-is-not-about-showing-diversity-of-mormon-beliefs/

Kernberg, O. Borderline Conditions and Pathological Narcissism. Aronson. 1975.

Kohut, H. How Does Analysis Cure? Eds. A. Goldberg and P.E Stepansky. Chicago. 1984.

LDS http://www.ldschurchnews.com/articles/58411/Use-proper-sources.html

Levy, R.A., Ablon, J.S., and Kachele, H. Psychodynamic Psychotherapy Research: Evidence-Based Practice and Practice-Based Evidence. Springer. 2012.

Miller, A. For Your Own Good: Hidden Cruelty in Cbild-Rearing and the Roots of Violence. Trans. H. and H. Hannum. Farrar, Straus, and Giroux. 1983.

Morain, W.D. The Sword of Laban: Joseph Smith, Jr., and the Dissociated Mind. APA. 1998.

O'Donovan, C. "The Abominable and Detestable Crime Against Nature: A Revised History of Homosexuality and Mormonism, 1840-1980." http://www.connellodonovan.com/abom.html

Pareene, A. "The Book of Mitt." Salon. 05-06-2012.

Russell, T. A Renegade History of the United States. Free Press. 2010.

Smith, L.M. Biographical Sketches of Joseph Smith the Prophet and His Progenitors for Many Generations. Liverpool. 1853. (Suppressed by Brigham Young.)

Stack, P.F. "Mormon church traces black priesthood ban to Brigham Young. Salt Lake Tribune. 12-11-13.

St. John of the Cross, "The Ascent of Mount Carmel." Trans. H. Hagius. In Pen.

St. John of the Cross. The Collected Works of St. John of the Cross. Trans. K. Kavanaugh and O. Rodriguez. , ICS. 1979.

Vogel, D. Joseph Smith: The Making of a Prophet (A Biography). Signature. 2004.
Walker, K.R. BYU%20View.webarchive

Wittgenstein, L. On Certainty. Trans. G.E.M. Anscombe and G.H.vW. Harpercollins. 1986.

Wittgenstein, L. Philosophical Investigations. Trans. G.E.M. Anscombe. Macmillan. 1953.

Zimmer, H. The King and the Corpse. Ed. J. Campbell. Princeton. 1946/1975.

THE OLD AND THE NEW

There is a crack in everything;
That's how the light gets in.

--Leonard Cohen

The shift in sensibility from modern to post-modern views has been discussed in academic circles for some time. The Enlightenment outlook has been unable to reflect our evolving sensibilities. In addition to its stress on the essential autonomy of individuals, this outlook has two troubling problems. One is its tendency to speak in lofty-sounding generalities. "All men are created equal." Sure. Sure they are. (Just men?) "Science will provide the answers." Sure again. Any day. To our ears the notion that knowledge and reason will lead to "the good" is almost laughable. (Well maybe *someday*, or perhaps *in principle*.)

The second problem is a continued development of and reliance on principles of power. Thus while the autocratic power of the church and land owners was opposed, power that could inhere in science and group politics continued.

The French philosopher Lyotard (1979/1984) defined post-modernism as that which is opposed to the "Grand Narratives" of the past. "I define *postmodern* as incredulity toward meta-narratives (Lyotard 1984, xxiv)." Thus, over-arching themes that define academic pursuits and culture are to be opposed. Further such generalities are notorious for eliding significant differences between individuals--which we all are. Psychologists have long known you cannot accurately deduce information about an individual subject from group data--and then they routinely go ahead and do it anyway (the ipsitive data problem).

334

The Enlightenment dream was that reason would rise and assert itself against chaos. This would issue in a society of order and well being. The problem with this approach is that in placing such stress on order, genuine expression tended to be crowded out or devalued. Nonetheless enlightenment principles became enshrined and dominant.

The ways that modern societies go about creating categories labeled as "order" or "disorder" have to do with the effort to achieve stability. Francois Lyotard... equates that stability with the idea of "totality," or a totalized system (think here of Derrida's idea of "totality" as the wholeness or completeness of a system). Totality, and stability, and order, Lyotard argues, are maintained in modern societies through the means of "grand narratives" or "master narratives," which are stories a culture tells itself about its practices and beliefs. A "grand narrative" in American culture might be the story that democracy is the most enlightened (rational) form of government, and that democracy can and will lead to universal human happiness. Every belief system or ideology has its grand narratives, according to Lyotard; for Marxism, for instance, the "grand narrative" is the idea that capitalism will collapse in on itself and a utopian socialist world will evolve. You might think of grand narratives as a kind of meta-theory, or meta-ideology, that is, an ideology that explains an ideology (as with Marxism); a story that is told to explain the belief systems that exist (Klages, 2003).

In terms of power, many decisions may be said to be made not so much based on creative thinking or reasonable plausibility, but by power of those who hold it. Though science, order and rationality were considered ideal (instead of religious fiat), power was seen as an acceptable means of insuring these things. Top down power as well as authoritarianism, however, is anathema to the postmodern outlook regardless of its region of origin.

The disrespect in which this approach to life is held is richly earned in the unending range of human misery it has spawned.

Modernity [which postmodern-ism opposes] is fundamentally about order: about rationality and rationalization, creating order out of chaos. The assumption is that creating more rationality is conducive to creating more order, and that the more ordered a society is, the better it will function (the more rationally it will function). Because modernity is about the pursuit of ever-increasing levels of order, modern societies constantly are on guard against anything and everything labeled as "disorder," which might disrupt order. Thus modern societies rely on continually establishing a binary opposition between "order" and "disorder," so that they can assert the superiority of "order." But to do this, they have to have things that represent disorder"--modern societies thus continually have to create/construct "disorder." In western culture, this disorder becomes "the other"--defined in relation to other binary oppositions. Thus anything non-white, non-male, non-heterosexual, non-hygienic, non-rational, (etc.) becomes part of "disorder," and has to be eliminated from the ordered, rational modern society (Ibid, see also Foucault, 1990).

Thus the eradication of disorder would leave only (rational) order. The virtue of this is that one would not have to grapple with the anxiety that order and disorder constantly create by their ongoing conflict--thereby issuing in a more peaceful existence.

Rationality has its own problems. According to the argumentative theory of reasoning, reason has routinely been used in the service of power in order to win arguments. It has rarely, if ever, been used in the dispassionate search for truth.

For centuries thinkers have assumed that the uniquely human capacity for reasoning has existed to let people reach beyond mere perception and reflex in the search for truth. Rationality allowed a solitary thinker to blaze a path to philosophical, moral and scientific enlightenment. Now some researchers are suggesting that reason evolved for a completely different purpose: to win arguments. Rationality, by this yardstick (and irrationality too, but we'll get to that) is nothing more or less than a servant of the hard-wired compulsion to triumph in the debating arena. According to this view, bias, lack of logic and other supposed flaws that pollute the stream of reason are instead social adaptations that enable one group to persuade (and defeat) another.

Certitude works, however sharply it may depart from the truth (Cohen, 2011).

Enlightenment thinking essentially shifted the power base from religion to reason, politics, and science. Yet, though the changes were significant at this juncture, power continued to be a central and highly significant factor.

In this light it is important to recall that in psychoanalysis the therapeutic strategy employed to treat anxiety is to analyze the ambivalence present in the conflict itself instead of pushing for an arbitrary choice to be made between conflicting positions. The pre-modern period sought to reduce anxiety by fostering adherence to religious dogma, and the modern period sought to reduce anxiety by the imposition of order and rational solutions. It is necessary in the post-modern period to remain with and manage the anxiety that comes with uncertainty. This is much harder to do. But it is also more likely to approximate the actual situation.

Focusing away from universal truths and authoritarianism, the new era could attempt to direct itself more toward alternatives to the use of power and the over-stress of rationality--which infused the modern system (see especially Foucault, 1965, 1994).

Argued Flax (1990):

> It is no longer self-evident that there
> is any necessary connection be-
> tween reason, knowledge, science,
> freedom, and human happiness. In-
> deed, the relation between these
> now appears to be at least partially
> and irresolvably antagonistic (p. 8).

Such ideas are having a difficult time being embraced by the larger culture, grounded as it is in
Enlightenment rhetoric, law, and formal religion.

The Enlightenment was a triumph over "antiqui-
ty" in that it sought to banish religious tyranny and
"magic" and replace it with reason. Belief was to
be replaced by science. Rational processes would
prevail. At the same time socially, however, rapid
industrialization ushered in new major abuses of
power. Workers, in many cases, were considered
to be chattel. The tyranny of the pulpit was replaced by the tyranny of the corporation. People
were crushed.

Epistemology was grounded in the "objective" study of "facts," objects, and data. Heisenberg was not yet on the scene. The Rosenthal effect or the "decline effect" (see below) were not yet known.

In fact the "objective" account of "facts" in the world was considered the appropriate domain of science and knowledge.

Foucault (1966) shattered conceptions of science's superior objectivity with his "archeology" of the sciences. He demonstrated quite clearly that the questions asked by scientists, the methodology used to study such questions, and the conclusions drawn from the resulting data were all colored by the time and place in which the experiment took place (see also Fausto-Sterling, 2000).

Recent studies bear this out.

In the late nineteen-nineties, John Crabbe, a neuroscientist at the Oregon Health and Science University, conducted an experiment that showed how unknowable chance events can skew tests of replicability. He performed a series of experiments on mouse behavior in three different science labs: in Albany, New York, Edmonton, Alberta, and Portland, Oregon. Before he conducted the experiments, he tried to standardize every variable he could think of. The same strains of mice were used in each lab, shipped on the same day from the same supplier. The animals were raised in the same kind of enclosure, with the same brand of saw dust bedding. They had been exposed to the same amount of incandescent light, were living with the same number of litter mates, and were fed the exact same type of chow pellets. When the mice were handled, it was with the same kind of surgical glove, and when they were tested it was on the same equipment, at the same time in the morning.

The premise of this kind of test of replicability, of course, is that each of the labs should have generated the same pat-tern of results. "If any set of experiments should have passed the test, it should have been ours," Crabbe says. "But that's not the way it turned out." In one experiment, Crabbe injected a particular strain of mouse with cocaine. In Portland the mice given the drug moved, on average, six hundred centimeters more than they normally did; in Albany they moved seven hundred and one additional centimeters. But in the Edmonton lab they moved more than five thousand additional centimeters. Similar deviations were observed in a test of anxiety. Furthermore, these inconsistencies didn't follow any detectable pattern. In Portland one strain of mouse proved most anxious, while in Albany another strain won that distinction (Lehrer, 2010, p. 57).

Lehrer pointed out these results point to little more than "noise."

As a result of such observations, it now seems obvious that what one is able to see depends in a large part on the assumptions one has as well as where one is standing when one sees. That is, the context is always significant.

If minute elements in the context are significant, generalities become less credible.

The crux of this problem can be seen in the Enlightenment view that the object of study is *reality*, that is: the objects and phenomena of our world. Further, our knowledge systems were held to be *independent* of these objects and are, thus, able to describe them objectively.

Postmodern views consider "objective perception" to be a personal construction.

The situation for "objective" science is even worse.

The magnitude of carefully achieved results has shown a tendency to drop as original experiments are replicated. This "decline effect" is common and troubling to scientific methodology.

> Michael Jennions, a biologist at the Australian NationalUniversity, set out to analyse "temporal trends" across a wide range of subjects in ecology and evolutionary biology. He looked at hundreds of papers and forty-four meta-analyses (that is, statistical syntheses of related studies), and discovered a consistent decline effect over time, as many of the theories seemed to fade into irrelevance. In fact, even when numerous variables were controlled for...there was still a significant decrease in the validity of the hypothesis, often within a year of publication (Ibid, p. 54).

Replacing the view of the immutability of "objective" observation is the notion of the "given" and the "made." The given is what is presented to us, i.e., the objects. The made is how we interpret or describe them--what significance they may have for us.

Thus how we interpret what we see is a function of what we know, our particular position in space and time when we see, our command of language, and other factors.

Postmodernism is largely a reaction to the assumed certain-ty of 'scientific, or objective, efforts to explain reality. In essence, it stems from a recognition that reality is not simply mirrored in human understanding of it, but rather, is constructed as the mind tries to understand its own particular and personal reality. For this reason, post-modernism is highly skeptical of explanations which claim to be valid for all groups, cultures, traditions, or races, and instead focuses on the relative truths of each person. In the postmodern understanding, interpretation is everything; reality only comes into

being through our interpretations of
what the world means to us individually (PBS).

Further, it is precisely these interpretations and
their descriptions that form our knowledge.
Knowledge must be communicated.   Thus language moves to center stage. Rorty (1978) argued
"there is no way to think about either the world or
our purposes except by using our language (p. 60;
see also Wittgenstein, *passim*)."   Further, when
one moves from the given to the made, it is clear
one is moving from objects to interpretations
(constructions). Thus knowledge is constructed by
our descriptions--which heavily depend upon our
language capacity.

(Obviously, having a language makes it impossible to imagine what it would be like not having a
language.)

There can be no (practical) thought
without language, and thought within the [post] modern world has no
practical effect without being trans-

formed into writing or texts that are "disseminated." Hence there is no world outside the text (Flax, p190; see also Derrida, 1974).

This shift from the given to the made is profound and affects all areas of inquiry. Further, Wittgenstein suggested language errors and misstatements can render descriptions we make nonsensical. Thus: good experiment + lousy account = flawed knowledge.

Also:

Intrinsic to traditional philosophy is the demand to "give reasons," to offer a set of arguments for why x is better than y. It is precisely this sort of discourse that postmodernism seeks to displace...The [postmodern] strategy is to construct an alternative narrative whose rhetorical force is to displace the traditional self-understanding of mainstream western thought (Ibid, pp. 194-95).

This change of method is extremely important. Instead of arguing or supplying evidence within the *same framework* as the problem has been conceived, the newer approach is to seek a view from a *different framework*. That is, issues routinely appear different when seen from a different perspective or frame of reference.

Thus, much as suggested in Wittgenstein's *Philosophical Investigations*, the procedure resembles psychotherapy more than it resembles traditional argument or logic. The solution does not resemble a specific answer so much as the overcoming of the problem by means of a different or more informed view.

Again,

> Postmodernists claim the construction and choice of one story over others is not governed by a relation to truth, but by less innocent factors. These ultimately include *a will to power* partially constituted by and

expressing a desire not to hear certain other voices or stories (Ibid.)
[my italics].

Thus in a similar way to how Enlightenment principles ignored the voices of non-European cultures, some views have became popular and accepted--even within rigorous circles--while others have been shunned. Certain books and journal articles have been published, and others denied. This has often not been primarily the workings of reason or clear narrative. It has been simply the workings of power.

To this day editorial preferences, regional attitudes and traditions, social fads, political allegiances, &c. figure to a substantial degree in what viewpoints become accepted and maintained.

Lyotard (1984) has even suggested that the optimum means of transferring information in our time is the computer. Knowledge, thus, becomes that which can accurately be conveyed by computerized applications.

In art, literature, and film there is a shift from recognizable works to more abstract expression. During the early part of the twentieth century artists frequently mourned the loss of certainty and order in culture.

An example from literature is the following by Yeats:

Turning and turning in the widening gyre
The falcon cannot hear the falconer,
Things fall apart; the centre cannot hold;
Mere anarchy is loosed upon the world,
The blood-dimmed tide is loosed, and
   everywhere
The ceremony of innocence is drowned;
The best lack all conviction, while the worst
Are full of passionate intensity.

Surely some revelation is at hand;
Surely the Second Coming is at hand.
The Second Coming! Hardly are these
   words out
When a vast image out of *Spiritus Mundi*
Troubles my sight: somewhere in sands of
   the desert

A shape with lion body and the head of a
   man,
A gaze blank and pitiless as the sun,
Is moving its slow thighs, while all about it
Reel shadows of the indignant desert birds.
The darkness drops again; but now I know
That twenty centuries of stony sleep
Were vexed to nightmare by a rocking
   cradle,
And what rough beast, its hour come round
   at last,
Slouches towards Bethlehem to be born?
(1921)

This beautifully conveys the sense of an "unraveling center," a breaking down of tradition. Such was the view from Yeats' time. It is not clear, however, from the viewpoint of (almost) a hundred years that the "rough beast" would be interested in slouching toward *Bethlehem*. I would imagine a new place, not yet imagined.

During the second half of the twentieth century a more playful attitude with abstraction and chaos was observed.

One of my own favorite pieces of art is the painting "OOF" in the Museum of Modern Art in New York City. This is a trio of yellow block letters against a navy blue background. That's it. Its playful sensibility is sheer delight.

The glee at thumbing one's nose at modern views has issued in a new freedom of expression as well as range of activity.

Another problem found in Enlightenment thinking has been a tendency to use polarization and binary categories. Thus there is a polarity between, for example, good and bad, rationality and irrationality, order and disorder, &c. Each of these antimonies tend to exclude serious consideration of the opposite or other. Further, a centering on the rational tends to limit the focus to the self, thus erasing an adequate understanding of the *other*.

Since Socrates, Western philosophy... "has always neutralized the other, in every sense of the word." Western philosophies have, thus, been philosophies of violence or philosophies of power. In its sup-

pression, exclusion, and transformation of the Other to the Same, "the
entire philosophical tradition, in its
meaning and at bottom, would make
common cause with oppression...
(Flax, p. 196).

As a result of this treatment, the "other" often
seems cast as something to be conquered or mas-
tered instead of something to be understood and
embraced.

In this way Enlightenment views essentially
omitted women. Hard as it may be to imagine,
deleting reference to roughly fifty percent of all
people was not thought to be a major problem.
Simply stated: some people mattered, and some
people did not. Further the so-called masculine
virtues of reason, order, and law were valorized
over so-called feminine virtues such as empathy,
nurturance, and interpersonal connection.

Since reason was a quality attributed to men,
they clearly were the Enlightenment ideal.

"All men are created equal." The implication is clear: these were *people*. I'm not sure what women were, but one senses they were certainly less. They weren't even smart enough to vote or hold property let alone make life and death decisions about their own bodies.

Further this arrangement of priorities took place in spite of the clear need for so-called feminine virtues, especially empathic resonance, in the maintenance of life and the development of healthy human beings.

Psychology itself began in an Enlightenment sensibility. It will be remembered how hard Freud struggled to have his psychoanalysis regarded as a scientifically respectable enterprise. It is telling that Freud, who otherwise was an astute and sensitive observer, simply accepted the social notions of his time concerning women. This likely suggests the question of the status of women was simply not thought something that needed consideration.

With further studies in feminism, it has been suggested that a major reason for the omission of consideration for women is the desire of men to retain a power advantage in society (see Goldner, 2002; Butler, 1999, 2004; Irigaray, 1985, 1985; et al). Granting women equal ranking diminishes that power and is thus resisted.

The new period regards the relegation of women to secondary status as abhorrent. Furthermore perpetuating a social order in which women are required (and restricted) to operate in specifically masculine terms is certainly less than ideal. This is especially true with the influx of women into graduate and professional schools (where they are seen to excel). Especially in such contexts there is *no* justification for unequal treatment based on sex (or anything else, for that matter, other than ability and contribution).

As they say, the cow still isn't back in the barn. The structure to enable women to be considered as full-fledged human beings in their own right has appeared more from studies in feminism and psychoanalysis than it has from postmodernism. At any rate, until women are included as full equals in our conceptual accounts, those accounts will be flawed and inadequate.

With the shift from Enlightenment sensibilities, the notion of a coherent development of human thought and culture has also been surpassed. Foucault (1977) suggested culture and thought advanced though the conflict generated by "heterogeneous elements that cannot be assimilated ." Thus, it is through discourse produced by disparate arguments that positions emerge. According to Foucault, moving backward to origins does not result in an ever more simple, more (logically) coherent concept. On the contrary, moving back leads to chaos, fragmentation, and disparity. So much for solid (or rational) underpinnings.

This implies the foundation of all knowledge rests in a kind of "injustice." According to Foucault what survives and flourishes is more the workings of power than anything else.

The problem is that this system (wittingly or unwillingly) deletes voices not approved. These voices, Foucault referred to somewhere as "subjugated discourses." They are the viewpoints of the poor, the disenfranchised, women, people of color, children and students--in short: "the other" (die Anderen).

The result is we continue to have access to *limited* views and certain (approved) viewpoints. Sometimes noted work must wait beyond its own time for attitudes to change enough to recognize its contribution.

The fear is (as articulated by Yeats above) that without the tether of a solid system, there will be chaos. And...chaos is, after all, *bad*. (It lacks order.) Whether or not chaos in fact results, one thing that will likely appear without such a tether is a wider selection. There will be less "TRUTH" and more "truth."

Still, it is not at all clear that reason, science, and (imposed) order has led to more *humanity*. It may even be argued that enforcement has surpassed considerations of the human. Similar casualties have been inclusion, compassion, help, empathy (not only for the *same*), allegiance to the group in addition to the self, &c.

Voice ends up being a vital component. It is important every voice be heard. Taking away one's voice takes away one's humanity. For similar reasons the first thing an invading force routinely does is to knock out the media. Then no one knows what is going on. Too many voices have been silenced for too long. These especially include those of women, the poor, the disenfranchised, the ridiculous, and the ugly.

It is not that these voices need to hold sway, but it is essential that they be included.

The direction that seems to be most promising is not the search for "truth" or consensual power in an Enlightenment fashion. It is, rather, an honest uttering of one's perspective along with the hope that it might be heard somewhere, and conversation will be possible.

Like an analyst in session, we might strive to hear what we have not been able to hear before.

Such a suggestion sounds easy enough. But it requires us to become more aware of the ways in which our own understanding is influenced and skewed according to our limited experience, location, and capacity. Seeing what one sees is easy; seeing what one does not see is the "real trick."

Limited experience coupled with the Freudian concepts of pre-conscious and unconscious dimensions both work to undermine the notion of one's own clarity of perception as well as the reasoned bases of his or her behavior. Freud's idea has ushered in the view that one's consciousness is severely limited and incomplete--scarcely a foundation for an adequate notion of reality.

Consequently, notions of the "self" in the post modern period are seen as constructions of idiosyncratic experiences and understandings. Further, in opposition to the Enlightenment view that the self was insular and individual, more recent views consider the self to be a construction within a profoundly affective interpersonal matrix (see Gabbard, 2000; Kohut, 1984; Benjaman, 1988, 1995; et al). One is a self in relation to others (including those in one's mind). One is not a self in isolation.

Problems in the self are created in relationships. It is therefore a tenet of analysis that the solution to be found will be within a (corrective) relationship. In this process empathy and emotional support are seen to be as important as reason and clarity.

This leaves the problems of power and justice. These dimensions present especially difficult issues for the post modern period where pluralism and pragmatism are stressed.

Specifically, how will it be possible to include all voices? How will we hear the timid and the malformed amid the eloquent and dominant? Are all voices *always* necessary? If not, when and where? How will we move beyond the insularity and polarization of groups? Is it even possible to move beyond a culture governed by wealth and power to one governed by humane ideas? What would that even look like? And of course there is always the issue of who is to decide?

In sum what has been occurring during our time may be thought of as a giant paradigm shift. *Priorities* have shifted. Enlightenment principles thought to be humane have been found wanting on those very grounds. The world of today is not the Enlightenment world. Reason is valuable but so is empathy. The viewpoint and talent of men is valuable but so is that of women. Disenfranchising the poor, the sick, and the unlucky in the service of applauding the rich and capable is not humane.

Justice and equality cannot be successfully granted to groups instead of to individuals. It is important to create channels to allow all voices to be heard, not just certain voices. The practice of wholesale privileging of men and male sensibility must give way to equal inclusion of women and female sensibility--compromised though it may be by long periods of male dominance.

But easily the most difficult issue to be considered will be a more humane solution to the problem of power. Routinely the product of feelings of inadequacy, power may bolster the self, but this is all too frequently at the expense of others. Power is also widely modeled in families and in schools. These are major shaping experiences.

For a variety of reasons, options to power will likely first emerge among those capable of tolerating significant ambiguity and uncertainty. The exclusion of female, homosexual, and other disenfranchised voices must end. We simply must get serious about realizing an empathic, tolerant, and truly loving environment.

Finally, these comments are to be considered *directions* toward awareness, not utopian and idealistic outcomes to be achieved. As Camus argued in The Plague: our greatest efforts will not make this a world in which innocent children do not suffer and die. But we *can* reduce the number of suffering children. We can do it ourselves.

REFERENCES

Benjamin J. The Bonds of Love: psychoanalysis, feminism, and the problem of domination. Pantheon, 1988.

Benjamin, J. Like Subjects, Love Objects: essays on recognition and sexual difference. Yale, 1995.

Butler, J. Gender Trouble, Routledge, 1999.

Butler, J. "Melancholy Gender-Refused Identification." In Gender In Psychoanalytic Space: between clinic and culture. (Eds.) M. Dimen, and V. Goldner. Other, 2002.

Butler, J. Undoing Gender. Routledge, 2004.

Camus, A. The Plague. Random House, 1948.

Cavell, S. Must We Mean What We Say? Cambridge, 1969.

Cohen, P. "Reason Seen More as Weapon Than Path to Truth." New York Times. 06-14-2011.

Derrida, J. Of Grammatology, Corrected Edition. Hopkins, 1974.

Fausto-Sterling, A. Sexing the Body: gender politics and the sexing of the body. Basic, 2000.

Flax, J. Thinking Fragments: psychoanalysis, feminism, and postmodernism in the contemporary west. California, 1990.

Foucault, M. Madness and Civilization. Random House, 1965.

Foucalt, M. "Truth and Power," in Foucault, M. Power/Knowledge. (Ed.) C. Gordon. Pantheon, 1980.

Foucault, M. "The Discourse on Language," in Foucault, M. Power/Knowledge, (ed.) C. Gordon. Pantheon, 1980.

Foucault, M. The History of Sexuality: an introduction. Vol. I. Vintage, 1990.

Foucault, M. The Order of Things: an archeology of the human sciences. Vintage, 1994.

Gabbard, G.O. Psychodynamic Psychiatry: in clinical practice. Third Edition. APA, 2000.

Goldner, V."Toward a Critical Relational Theory of Gender," in Gender in Psychoanaoytic Space: between clinic and culture. (Eds.) M. Dimen and V. Goldner. Other, 2002.

Irigaray, L. Speculum of the Other Woman. Cornell, 1985.

Irigaray, L. This Sex Which Is Not One. Cornell, 1985.

Johnson, J. http://www.albany.edu/~jej84/Dickinson/alterity.htm

Klages, M. http://www.colorado.edu/English/courses/ENGL2012Klages/pomo.html 2003.

Kohut, H. How Does Analysis Cure? (Ed.) A. Goldberg. Chicago, 1984

Lehrer, J "The Truth Wears Off: an odd twist in the scientific method." New Yorker, 12-30-10, pp. 52-57.

Lyotard. J-F. The Postmodern Condition: a report on knowledge. Minnesota, 1984.

PBS.   www.pbs.org/faithandreason/gengloss/postm-body.html

Pitcher, G. The Philosophy of Wittgenstein. Prentice-Hall, 1964.

Rorty, R. "Pragmatism," in Bayes, K., Bohman, and McCarthty, T.   After Philosophy: End or Transformation? MIT, 1978.

Thody, P.   Albert Camus: a study of his work. Grove, 1957.

Wittgenstein, L.   Philosophical Investigations. (Trans.) G.E.M. Anscombe. Macmillan, 1953.

Wittgenstein, L.   The Blue and Brown Books. Blackwell, 1958.

Wittgenstein, L. Tractatus Logico Philosophicus. (Trans. D.F. Pears and B.F. McGuinnes. Routledge, 1961.

Wittgenstein, L. On Certainty. (Eds.) G. E. M. Anscombe and G.H. von Wright. Blackwell, 1969.

Yeats, W. B. "The Second Coming," in The Collected Poems of W.B. Yeats. (Ed.) Finneran, R. J. Macmillan, 1983, pp. 187-18

FORMS OF LIFE

Thought can as it were *fly*,
it doesn't have to walk.

--Ludwig Wittgenstein
Zettel (273)

Developments in the philosophy of language and postmodernism have focused on improved views of how language works as well as the importance of the context in perceptions.

371

These developments suggest important issues for psychoanalysis and psychotherapy. There are two areas in which this is so. First is the notion of meaning as use, and second is the notion of the grammatical context as the ground of human understanding.

Specifically, the strategy employed in learning about things has shifted.

Anderson stated:

> Dating from the Enlightenment and Descartes, the modern paradigm is based on the belief that a cognizing self can use reason and knowledge to under-stand and manipulate an objectively verifiable world. The postmodern paradigm abandons the individual-world duality and makes a radical move to a sociolinguistic frame. In the postmodern view, reality--even so called scientific reality--is woven and rewoven on shared linguistic looms (p. xii).

If understanding is enabled and constituted by language, it becomes all the more important to have an adequate grasp of how language works.

The paradigm shift is as follows: In the modern way of thinking 1) there were observers and objects or facts in the world, and 2) knowledge of the world was attained by the observers studying and manipulating those objects or facts. In the postmodern way of thinking, both of the above principles have been rejected. These have been replaced by: 1) the observers and the objects or facts are essentially not separable [*Dasein*], and 2) the way to understand the world is by understanding the *grammar* of the language.

This shift is illustrated quite clearly by the differences in the work of the early and later Wittgenstein.

In Tractatus Logico-Philosophicus (1961) Wittgenstein's view may be stated as follows:

The world is represented by thought, which is a proposition with sense, since they all—world, thought, and proposition—share the same logical form. Hence, the thought and the proposition can be pictures of the facts (Biletzki, and Matar, 2011).

And:

> Explaining that "Only the proposition has sense; only in the context of a proposition has a meaning" (*TLP* 3.3), he provides the reader with the two conditions for sensical language. First, the structure of the proposition must conform with the constraints of logical form, and second, the elements of the proposition must have reference (*bedeutung*) (Ibid.).

Here the view is that language refers to objects and facts in the world. Further it is this reference that gives propositions (language) meaning. We may say language points to things. We learn the words by pointing to the objects to which they refer (ostensive definition).

In his later work, Wittgenstein (1953) questioned the notion of language as a picture of things, largely learned ostensively ("naming"). That is, thinking that language "applied" to "things." He instead thought of 1) linguistic elements and 2) what those elements could be used, on a particular occasion, to accomplish (see also Bower, 2011). An example he used was tools in a toolbox. Here, the tools themselves are the elements, and what those tools are used to do on a particular occasion is the use. For example, we may use the hammer to hold the door open. It is important here to notice that focusing on the tool itself cannot tell us what it was used on a particular occasion to accomplish.

For that we must focus on the context of the use.

> For a large class of cases--though not for all--in which we employ the word "meaning" it can be defined thus: the meaning of a word is its use in the language. (PI, 43)

Thus speaking a language consists of 1) knowing the elements of the language, and 2) knowing how to use those elements on a specific occasion to accomplish something.

Wittgenstein made the analogy with tools explicit.

> Think of the tools in a tool-box: there is a hammer, pliers, a saw, a screw-driver, a rule, a glue-pot, glue, nails and screws.—The functions of words are as diverse as the functions of these objects. (And in both cases there are similarities.) (PI 11)

For example the patient says, "I feel terrible."

How would we begin to understand this statement? The answer is by gaining more information about the context from which, or in terms of which, the utterance was made, that is the specific use involved.

Similarly, if a man were running down a street screaming "Pencil!" We would not know what this means, because we would not have enough context--that is: what could be involved.

It occurred to Wittgenstein to compare language use to games.

In his memoir of Wittgenstein, Malcolm (1954) stated:

> One day when Wittgenstein was passing a field where a football game was in progress the thought first struck him that in language we plays games with words. A central idea of his philosophy, the notion of a 'language-game', apparently had its genesis in this incident (p. 65).

Wittgenstein's later thought may be stated as follows:

[For Wittgenstein]...words are not pictures, but pieces used in various language-games. And just as the significance of a piece in chess depends on its "role in the game" (PI, sect. 563)—i.e., how it can be moved, how one behaves with it—so the meaning of a word is its role in the various language-games in which it figures, the kind of behavior that surrounds its use, the kind of behavior in which its use is embedded. An expression only has meaning in —indeed only gets its meaning from —these modes of behavior. (Malcolm p. 93)

Also:

An expression has meaning only in the stream of life (Ibid. 93).

The consequence of this reasoning is that meaning is a function of *use*. One discovers the meaning by understanding the use. And use, of course, is a form of behavior. But it is not behavior in the abstract by any means. It is behavior within a specific or individual context. In an important sense, it is *both* the context in which the behavior occurs and the behavior itself that determine meaning. The behavior and the context cannot be "meaningfully" separated.

If for no other reason, it is critical for the analyst or therapist to understand as much as possible about the context in which a patient lives, thinks, feels, and understands in order to make sense of his or her behavior, thought processes, as well as psychological adjustments--including which language games he or she plays and why.

Further, for language games to be meaningful, they must not be arbitrary.

Wittgenstein said:

> It is not possible that there should have been only one occasion on which someone obeyed a rule. It is not possible that there should have

been only one occasion on which a report was made, or order given or understood; and so on.—To obey a rule, to make a report, to give an order, to play a game of chess are customs (uses, institutions). To understand a sentence means to understand a language. To understand a language means to be master of a technique. (PI 199)

Just as there is no universal person, so there is no universal language-game, and thus there is no one universally correct viewpoint. The individual person and the individual context differ from all others.

In this light one of the most far-reaching developments of Wittgenstein's thinking was his so-called "attack on essentialism." Thus we may ask what it is that trees have in common by virtue of which we call them "trees." We could, of course, ask what it is that frightened people have in common by virtue of which we call them frightened people.

To understand this issue, Wittgenstein focused on games.

Instead of producing something common to all that we call language, I am saying that these phenomena have no one thing in common which makes us use the same word for all,--but that they are *related* to one another in many different ways. And it is because of this relationship, or these relationships, that we call them all "language." I will try to explain this.

Consider for example the proceedings that we call "games". I mean board-games, card-games, ball-games, Olympic games, and so on. What is common to them all?-- Don't say: "There *must* be something common, or they would not be called 'games'"--but *look and see* whether there is anything common to all.--For if you look at them you will not see something that is com-

mon to *all*, but similarities, relationships, and a whole series of them at
that.   To repeat: don't think, but
look!--Look for example at board-
games, with their multifarious relationships. Now pass to card-games;
here you find many correspon-
dences with the first group, but
many common features drop out,
and others appear. When we pass
next to ball-games, much that is
common is retained, but much is
lost.-- Are they all 'amusing"?
Compare chess with noughts and
crosses [tic tac toe]. Or is there always winning and losing, or competition between players? Think of
patience. In ball games there is
winning and losing, but when a
child throws his ball at the wall and
catches it again, this feature has disappeared. Look at the parts played
by skill and luck; and at the difference between skill in chess and skill
in tennis. Think now of games like
ring-a-ring-a-roses; here is the element of amusement, but how many

other characteristic features have disappeared! And we can go through the many many other groups of games in the same way; can see how similarities crop up and disappear. And the result of this examination is: we see a complicated network of similarities overlapping and cross-crossing: sometimes overall similarities, sometimes similarities of detail. (PI 65,66)

Said Wittgenstein:

I can think of no better expression to characterize these similarities than "family resemblances"; for the various resemblances between members of a family: build, features, colour of eyes, gait, temperament, etc. etc. overlap and criss-cross in the same way.-- And I shall say: 'games' form a family. (PI 67)

The importance of this line of thought becomes more clear when we realize the search for general, underlying principles has long been the focus of science. Further, these underlying and general principles are typically thought to be the *causes* of the phenomena under consideration.

This issue was considered by Curry:

> When one asks a scientist about the nature of gravity, say, one is referred to further phenomena, variously to apparatuses and laws and institutions and practices. But, Wittgenstein is say-ing, at some point, we are *all* in the position of the parent faced with a two-year old who insists on asking 'Why?' If most people 'today stop at the laws of nature, treating them as something inviolable, just as God and Fate were treated in past ages' (TLP 3 6.372)' the scientist too is forced, in the end, to say, 'That's just how it is.' Or again,

'Then I am inclined to say: "This is simply what I do".' And when we say this, when we appeal to what we take to be the bedrock in our lives, we are appealing to 'what must be accepted', to 'forms of life'. So to say that a form of life, for Wittgenstein, must be accepted is just to say that something *becomes* a form of life by virtue of having that role, that function. Now it may seem that this is a transparent and unproblematic process: You ask me a series of probing questions about my actions, and at some point I say, 'This is just the way we do it around here,' or 'This is just the way we do it in our family,' or 'It's a women's thing.' (p. 106)

What is here suggested is that membership in a class is achieved via language and analogy, not essence. There is no thing all women have in common. No thing all jewelry, all broken hearts, all baseballs, all depressions, &c., have in common. They are related by the language-game that is used in specific instances concerning them. And all language-games have, at best, a family resemblance.

Wittgenstein said:

> And for instance the kinds of number form a family in the same way. Why do we call something a "number"? Well, perhaps because it has a—direct—relationship with several things that have hitherto been called number; and this can be said to give it an indirect relationship to other things we call the same name...But it someone wished to say: "There is something common to all these constructions—namely the disjunction of all their common properties"—I should reply: Now you are only playing with words. One might as well say: "Something runs through the whole thread—namely the continuous over-lapping of those fibres:. (PI 67)

Thus elements may belong together, though they don't have any underlying similarity--or, indeed, any underlying thing at all.

> Postmodernists argue that thought is irreducibly linguistic; it can be practiced only in and through historical and context-dependent "language games" or "discourses"...There is no reality for us outside such systems because, as Rorty argues, "there is no way to think about either the world or our purposes except by using language"...All language games generate their own rules about how to play, what counts as a successful move, and so forth. But by definition these rules are context dependent and valid only within a particular game. Games and their rules are incommensurable (Flax, 2000, p. 202)

The point here is that thought and being *human* are essentially tied up with language, and an understanding of that thought and humanity will likewise be linguistic.

The other point is that the world is understood through language, not through manipulation and study of objects, facts, or properties, whatever these might mean.

Furthermore, the nuance and complexity of thought and human experience requires a language that is itself capable of capturing that nuance and experience. Languages that seek to define or formalize descriptions of human language and behavior necessarily depart from, and thus distort, the spontaneously occurring ordinary language (i.e., operational definitions).

It may be objected the ordinary language is too complicated. But that complexity is important for the kinds of knowing sought in psychoanalysis and psychotherapy. Here we are trying to understand a person. And this involves trying to understand how a person functions in his/her context.

Thus "knowing" and "understanding" are linguistic enterprises, and psychotherapy consists of a kind of conversation and exchange between two language-users--each of whom have emerged from different formative contexts.

Heidegger said:

> We—mankind--are a conversation. The being of men is founded in language. But this only becomes actual in *conversation*. Nevertheless the latter is not merely a manner in which language is put into effect, rather it is only as conversation that language is essential. What we usually mean by language, namely a stock of words and syntactical rules, is only a threshold of language. (Heidegger 1965: 277)

Similarly, European philosophers have focused on the interweave of language and knowing (Foucault, 1970, Derrida, 1976, et al).

A friend suggested I read Thomas Ogden, so I plowed in and found him insightful and maddening. At one point I encountered the following:

> The autistic-contiguous position is understood as a sensory-dominated, pre-symbolic area of experience in which the most primitive form of meaning is generated on the basis of the organization of sensory impressions, particularly at the skin surface (1989, p. 4)

I read that passage again. I laid the book down and thought: "I'm in big trouble." Intrigued, however, by the language involved, I thought about it for considerable time. Finally I think I hit upon a way to translate the above into English.

> Before the acquisition of language the child has a kind of experience based on the skin and its immediate contact with other things.

I'm pretty sure my image of a baby cranking a grinder-like device with generated meanings flying out the front as one might generate electricity was not what Ogden meant by his poetic language.

It is not necessary to say one "generates meaning" to say, quite unambiguously, one "means."

Also it may be said there is a difference between "meaning" and "significance." For example: The word "airplane" may elicit a difference response from me, because, say, my sister was killed on one, than it elicits from you--who just like to ride on them. But in this case the word "airplane" has the same meaning--and it if didn't, we couldn't see it differently. That is we both know what the machine is we are taking about. The difference here is that the word airplane signifies a painful loss for me, whereas for you it signifies a quick way to get to, say, New York.

Often when we learn to "see things differently," we find a different significance for the same situation or experience (Ogden's sense of "meaning?").

One thing different significance does *not* suggest is that we all have our own meanings for words.

...for an utterance to be meaningful it must be possible in principle to subject it to public standards and criteria of correctness. For this reason, a private- language, in which "individual words ... are to refer to what can only be known to the person speaking; to his immediate private sensations ..."(PI 243), is not a genuine, meaningful, rule-governed language. The signs in language can only function when there is a possibility of judging the correctness of their use, "so the use of [a] word stands in need of a justification which everybody understands" *(PI* 261).

Wittgenstein adopts the term 'grammar' in his quest to describe the workings of this public, socially governed language, using it in a somewhat idiosyncratic manner

Grammar is usually taken to consist of the rules of correct syntactic and semantic usage, becomes, in Wittgenstein's hands, the wider—and more elusive—network of rules which determine what linguistic move is allowed as making sense, and what isn't. This notion replaces the stricter and purer logic which played such an essential role in the *Tractatus* in providing a scaffolding for language and the world. Indeed, "*Essence* is expressed by grammar ...Grammar tells what kind of object anything is. (Theology as grammar)" (*PI* 371, 373). The "rules" of grammar are not mere technical instructions from on-high for correct usage; rather, they express the norms for meaningful language. Contrary to empirical statements, rules of grammar describe how we use words in order to both justify and criticize our particular utterances. But as opposed to grammar-book rules, they are not idealized as an external system to be conformed to. Moreover, they are not appealed to explicitly in any formulation, but are used in cases of philosophical perplexity to clarify where language misleads us into false illusions. Thus, "I can know what someone else is thinking, not what I am thinking. It is correct to say 'I know what you are thinking', and wrong to say 'I know what I am thinking.' (A whole cloud of philosophy condensed into a drop of grammar.)" (*PI*, p.222). (Witt-1)

The "rules" being considered here are not rigid proscriptions from dusty grammar books that dictate strict obedience, but something more like "our consensus about how the game is played." Wittgenstein stressed:

It can be seen that there is a misunderstanding here from the mere fact that in the course of our argument we give one interpretation after another; as if each one contented us at least for **a** moment, until we thought of yet another standing behind it. What this shews is that there is a way of grasping a rule which is *not* an *interpretation,* but which is exhibited in what we call 'obeying the rule' and 'going against it' in actual cases. (PI 201)

Indeed, 'To obey a rule, to make a report, to give an order, to play a game of chess, are *customs*
(uses, institutions) *(PI* 199).'

Said Curry:

So in the end, we need to see that to obey a rule - in mathematics or language, chess or football or the workplace - is not - or not merely - to act in accord with the image. Rather, it is to do something within a broader social context. Rules are defined and maintained only as David Bloor (1997) has forcefully argued, within institutions. (Curry, 102)

Wittgenstein spoke of rules in many ways:

> To obey a rule, to make a report, to give an order, to play a game of chess, are *customs* (uses, institutions). To understand a sentence means to understand a language. To understand a language means to be master of a technique (PI 199)

> And hence also 'obeying a rule' is a practice. And to *think* one is obeying a rule is not to obey a rule. Hence it is not possible to obey a rule 'privately': otherwise thinking one was obeying a rule would be the same thing as obey-ing it. (PI 202)

> Following a rule is analogous to obeying an order. We are trained to do so; we react to an order in a par-

ticular way...The common behavior of mankind is the system of reference by means of which we interpret an unknown language. (PI 206)

In stressing the importance of rules in language and meaning, Wittgenstein focused on the (mistaken) tendency we have to want to get "outside" language in order to establish, say, an "objective" view. He also commented at length on the chaos that results when language is pulled beyond its ordinary duties.

[Wittgenstein] is concerned about the propensity that people have to extend the application of concepts beyond their legitimate scope - and then to be puzzled by the results. This often happens when we are misled by grammatical similarities among statements. *So,* for example, from the fact that I can say 'I have a tooth-ache' and 'I have your book,' we imagine that we ought to be able to say 'I have your toothache' and are puzzled about a person's relationship to his or her body when that statement makes no sense. Similarly, we imagine that we can go from 'People seek happiness' to 'Plants seek light,' with no problems. A second area of concern was the propensity to create reified abstractions. Certainly central here was the way in which people commonly go from the assertion that words have meanings to the assertion that there must be some-thing *called* a meaning, that exists somewhere 'out there'. We imagine that because we can talk about 'equilibrium' or 'capital', that they must be things that somehow exist in the world. Or from 'I think' we conclude that there must be an 'I' that thinks. (Curry p. 105)

In summary, then, the above comments suggest intellectual enterprises have long overlooked or exceeded the language they have been using. It is as if we thought we were describing the world, but what we were really describing were the window-panes through which we see the world. Ignoring language and a sensible description of how it works has led us to think of "meaning" as a "thing" that goes on in a "mind." Perhaps it is the result of a series of synapses that "cause" it. And if I am depressed, it is due to a mental illness that "caused" that.

And then there must be something common to expressions of phenomena, some essential principle we can isolate by means of random drug trials and empirical research.

Such views ignore the way language is used and can be meaningful. They also ignore the ways in which persons grow, learn, and develop psychological problems.

Wittgenstein said:

> "The general form of propositions is: 'This is how things are.'"—That is the kind of proposition that one repeats to oneself countless times.

One thinks that one is tracing the outline of the thing's nature over and over again, and one is merely tracing round the frame though which we look at it. (PI 114)

And:

A *picture* held us captive. And we could not get outside it, for it lay in our language and language seemed to repeat it to us inexorably. (PI 115)

This is a long way from the notion that words stand for things or are the names of things—or even that meaning is some "property" words "have." It is also a long step from the notion that "things" are primary in our understanding and words are pretty much an arbitrary afterthought.

Wittgenstein stressed:

We are trying to get hold of the mental process of under-standing which seems to be hidden behind... coarser and therefore more readily visible accompaniments. But we do not succeed, or, rather, it does not get as far as a real attempt. For even supposing I had found something that happened in all...cases of understanding,-- why should *it* be the understanding? And how can the process of understanding have been hidden, when I [say] "Now I understand" *because* I understood? And if I say it is hidden, then how do I know what I have to look for? I am in a muddle. (PI 153)

The issue has been made yet more complex by the views of postmodernism   (Gadammer, 1989, Foucault, 1970) in which a purely objective viewpoint is considered impossible. Each view is importantly influenced by the position from which the view is made. This has made it imperative that one state not only one's view but the position from

401

which the view was made. "Objective" science has "always been deeply influenced by the era in which it was produced--thus rendering it, of course, less than truly objective (see Fausto-Sterling, 2000).

Furthermore knowledge involves description, which is a linguistic enterprise *par excellence*. This has led to the view there is no reality beyond the text (Derrida, 1976, Lyotard, 1984). Thus if the description is wrong or limited, the knowledge will also be wrong or limited. As Eliot's Sweeny said: "I got to use words when I talk to you (1932)."

II.

It may seem strange to focus on explanations and other uses of language instead of "facts" and "things" that language may be used to talk about. But since conceptual understanding is essentially linguistic in character, and is--if you will--the "lens" through which "facts" and "things" may be understood, awareness is inexorably tied to language.

It is an implication of Wittgenstein's reasoning that: "If I could not speak the language, I could not see this tree."

This is not to say I could not make any discriminations whatsoever (pigeons can do that), but 1) I would have no device to separate the "tree-pattern" from the "surround pattern." Grammar is that device. In grammar, nothing can be wrong if it cannot also be right. 2) "Tree" is a word that I must know how to use correctly. 3) With language I have a conceptual device to link "tree" with a larger understanding.

Clearly language was the light that shinneth into the darkness. Without which not.

Even if we were to attempt to discover the "properties" of the tree, whatever that might mean, we must use language in such an enterprise.

The suggestion is that as infants we seek to learn about the environment in which we find ourselves. From the start we are in a human context that includes other people, movement, language, touch, &c. We are in an energy that is called human. Our movements are human movements, our speech is human speech, and our interpersonal interactions are of a human form.

This energy that forms the foundation for our experience is what Wittgenstein called a "form of life."

> What holds a form of life together is not only its linguistic practices but everything else that goes into that form of life: Human mortality, birth, social systems, mundane facts such as that we become tired and need rest, and so forth. What is involved in a form of life is therefore not a matter of belief, as it were something to be approximated, for example, to a set of sentences to which we assent or dissent. It is rather more like the *conditions* of there being any such thing as a belief at all; it is all of those things that go toward making up the background sense we carry

around with us about what, for example, the rule really does require of us, how we are to carry on in the right ways, and so on, which make possible the ways in which we form, evaluate, approve and reject beliefs. This "source" of sense-making is by no means "self-standing" but is instead itself always in movement (as Cavell's metaphor of the "whirl" of organism aptly expresses). A form of life in Wittgenstein's sense refers to...[a] "common mode of human action," including within itself more culturally qualified matters, such as kinships, rituals, and so forth. As a form of *life*, it thus has certain standards built into it in that, in being a mode of life, it can be defective in certain ways (such as being diseased); on Wittgenstein's view, so it seems, the standards built into the human form of life contain the "common modes of human action," the taken-for-granted background in terms of which what holds these practices together makes sense and which provide an unarticulated sense of standards for judging whether that *human* form of life is keeping faith with itself. However, built into the human condition is thus the ongoing temptation to ask what further holds that form of life itself together — to ask for the reasons behind the standards built into the form of life — and thus to be led to search for something external to those practices, the "invisible rails," on which they could be fitted. That temptation, however, is part of what must be resisted. Wittgenstein argued that when those kinds of questions are pushed to their extreme, the only proper response is to note that reason-giving has run out, and that the view that there simply *must be* further reasons for those reasons is to be diagnosed as succumbing to the illusion that there must be an external standpoint that would provide something else more normatively fundamental to which we could appeal; instead we should accept the fact that "if I have exhausted the justifications I have reached bedrock, and my spade is turned. Then I am inclined to say: "This is simply what I do'." On the reading being sketched, Wittgenstein's suggestion, in short, seems to be that our "form of life" is always "is in order as it is," and looking for anything outside of the practices that make up that form of life can only result in "nonsense." (Witt-2)

It is the fact we are part of the human form of life that allows us to learn about other humans. We can, for example, learn another language, because another language is as well a part of the human form of life.

Wittgenstein said: "If a lion could speak, we could not understand him (PI, p. 223)." This is so as we don't take part in the lion form of life. In other words we don't know how it is to live a lion's life.

Our language and customs are fixed not by laws so much as by what Wittgenstein calls "forms of life," referring to the social contexts in which language is used. In other words, the most fundamental aspect of language is that we learn how to use it in social contexts, which is the reason why we all understand each other. We do not understand each other because of a relationship between language and reality. Wittgenstein gives the example of a student who obeys the rule "add 2" by writing 1004 after 1000 and insisting that this is a correct application of the rule. In such an instance, there is nothing we can say or do to persuade the student otherwise because the misunderstanding lies at a deeper level than explanation can reach. Such examples do not occur in ordinary life not because there is some perfectly unambiguous explanation for "add2" but because we share forms of life: people, on the whole, simply understand one another, and if this basic understanding were miss-

ing, communication would be impossible. (Witt-3)

One may think of a university. One may think
of the kinds of things one might do, think, and feel
in a university setting. One may be said to be par-
ticipating in a university experience, one of the
ways to be human.

Angelo (2008) described a simple parable to il-
lustrate the concept of "form of life."

Imagine quite a different world (say,
sometime in some supposed evolu-
tionary past), one where everyone is
blind; no one's eyes work or have
ever worked. Then, one day a child
is born who can see. The child is
very good at certain games, say
chase ("blind man's bluff"). One day
the people go for a walk -- or rather,
an exploration — in a place where
they have never traveled before.
They walk in lines, of course, one
behind the other. The child suddenly

says, "There is a tree in front of you." And its mother responds:"Non-sense. You're behind me; how can you know that there's a tree in front of me (You haven't touched it)?" What can the child say? Certainly not 'I see it'. Those words have no place in these people's language. The child can only say 'I know ...', but *not* 'I know because I touched it'. And the mother responds that the words 'I know' cannot be used in these cir-cumstances. "I know there's a tree in front of you." --

"How do you know. What do you mean by 'I know'?" Asking whether or how a statement can be verified is only a particular way of asking 'How do you mean?' The answer is a con-tribution to the *grammar* of the statement. (*PI* § 353) Of course the people can -- both physically and grammatically -- verify that the tree is there. But they cannot verify that the child knows it is there. What can the child do other than guess. Per-

410

haps the child has been here before? But no one has been here before. It's a still day: you can't hear the branches shake or smell and taste the scent of the tree on the wind. And the sun isn't out, so the tree isn't blocking its warmth. The tree doesn't have surface roots either, nor are there leaves on the ground. "The child has no grounds for saying 'I know'", the people have the (grammatical) right to say. The mother instructs the child: "You have to touch the tree in this case to know." And all the people, each in their turn, can repeat this remark to the child. Perhaps they even play a "language-game" with the child. They take it by the hand, have it touch the tree, and say 'I know'. And perhaps they tell the child the story of "The Little Boy Who Cried Tree!" (This would be quite important to these people -- not walking into trees.) And, so, if the child knows only by seeing, for the people of this world it doesn't know at all – even if it "guesses" right

411

every time. Indeed, if the child "guesses" right too often, they may take it for a demon and kill it. If the child persisted in saying 'I know' in these circumstances, the mother might slap it. It is her responsibility to teach the child the people's language (Angelo 2008).

Wittgenstein had something like a basic human truth in mind when he thought about forms of life. Blair's (2006) list of related concepts included: background, background within human life, bustle of life, human behavior, circumstances, common behavior of mankind, natural history, pattern of life, weave of life, stream of life, occasions, activities, swirl of human actions, and This is simply what I do (p. 120)."

Further:

Someone says, "Religion is a form of life, but not one that I participate in." This sounds like a statement about elections such as that someone doesn't vote, as if this were entirely a matter of choice. But I do not think that this is what Wittgenstein meant by 'form of life'. A man may reject religious belief -- but only because religious belief is a human form of life. A dog cannot be an atheist or a believer; religion is not a canine form of life. That is why Wittgenstein talks about "our natural history": 'our form of life' concerns human nature. I believe that is why he wrote that if a dog [lion] could talk, we would not understand him (cf. ibid. II, xi, p. 223g), because of *differences in our forms of life.*

In thinking the form of life is the bedrock, say, one is indirectly saying the bedrock is not a *construct.* (Constructs arise, as it were, from forms of life.)

Such a position has important implications for understanding what is human.

III

In psychology we are taught that our behavior is a function of our personality structure. This "personality structure is constructed out of elements "internalized" from our surround. Our internal fundamental relationships are considered to be "object relations." Our behavior stems from erroneous "core beliefs" to which we cling as a foundation. We have "wired" problem behaviors and views, &c.

Our core beliefs and object relations are things in our "minds" if not in our "brains." Our "attachment patterns" are etched into our neural pathways, and these "etchings" cause our behavior in reliable patterns.

Such views swing on the notion *something is responsible* for our thoughts and behavior, something that, say, *underlies* our thoughts and behaviors. The goal of our studies is to uncover these *elements*. That is to say our efforts are on constructing theories about basic elements that produce the thought, feelings, and behavior that interests us.

In a way, this is a view based on a kind of architecture of elements (see Bower, 2011).

In contrast to this mode of operation, Wittgenstein is telling us it is grammar that tells us what anything is.

Shotter claimed:

> Rather than any realities as such determining our forms of life, it is the grammars of our forms of life - our inner sense of their relational structure - which determine for us what can possibly count as a reality within them. Thus, if we can come to a 'survey-able' grasp of the possibilities offered us by the grammars of our forms of life, it should be possible to become so well oriented within them, that one can see ahead of time, so to speak, what is possible within it (and what is not) (p.1).

In this view, behaviors, thoughts, and feelings emerge organically from forms of life.

> Like a city that one can only famil-
> iarize oneself with from one's in-
> volvements within it, so we must
> enter into it and explore its possibil-
> ities actively. This whole approach
> of Wittgenstein's contrasts markedly
> with our current approach in the so-
> cial and behavioral sciences. There,
> we usually follow what might be
> called the way of theory, with its
> central assumption of the *radical*
> *hiddenness of unitary sources*
> (Ibid.) [My italics].

These "unitary sources" that are "radically hidden" are assumed elements upon which theory construction proceeds. It is sometimes said, in fact, that understanding *requires* a theory.

Said Shotter:

416

If Wittgenstein (1953) is correct, all of our more self-conscious, individual activities have their being within a stream, or mingling streams, of spontaneously responsive activity flowing continuously between us, unnoticed in the background of our lives together...It cannot be explained either as behavior in terms of causes, not as action in terms of reasons. Until recently, this sphere of diffuse, sensuous or feelingful activity, this unordered hurly-burly or bustle of everyday social life, has remained unnoticed in the background to our lives. If we have noticed it at all, we have not attached much importance to it; we have assumed that it will one day all be explained in terms of timeless, yet to be discovered, orderly principles of mind and/or world. Central to the whole philosophy underlying this stance, is the assumption that everything should be understood in terms

417

of orderly systems. Thus our utterances have meaning only because they are linked in an orderly way with other kinds of events (with states of mind, states of affairs), otherwise, they would just be meaningless noises. Indeed, as Saussure (1959) claims in discussing speech, "Speaking…is an individual act. It is willful and intellectual" (p. 14); it can only be meaningful and understood by others if it is properly ordered by a speaker in a self conscious manner (pp 1,2).

Saussure and orderly systems aside, Wittgenstein's view suggests that interacting with others around us in a spontaneous and familiar way implies "this kind of activity between us is not yours nor mine but our's (Ibid). Further these exchanges are *out there* in "public space." Language arises out of our spontaneous "reactions" in the ongoing flux of people around us.

> The origin and primitive form of the language-game is a reaction; only from this can more complicated forms develop. Language--I want to say--is a refinement, 'in the beginning was the deed' (1980a, p. 31).

Again, this spontaneous interaction with others is ours.

Said Shotter:

> Thus, when I understand a person's speech, it is a matter of me responding to a public situation with the kind of publicly anticipated responses into which I have been trained. (p. 2)

And therefore:

> Here, then, we have two very different approaches to language and to

419

our intelligent, knowledgeable behavior. In one approach, running in a line from Descartes, through Saussure and Chomsky, all the way to current cognitive psychology, there is the view that our linguistic utterances can only be meaningful and understood by others if they are properly ordered, and we can only achieve this by explicitly or tacitly referring to an inner mental representation of a system of rules (our linguistic competence) in our performance of them. The other view is Wittgenstein's. As he remarks, we hardly ever speak in the self-conscious way required by the first approach, with such an inner, intellectual reference to a system of rules. Indeed, if we did self-consciously bring such a rule schematism to mind, we would still have to interpret how to apply it in this, that, or another specific situation. And where might we find the rules to do that? In finding ourselves in a situation which seems to require a certain kind of appropriate response from us, simply stating a rule doesn't seem of much help to us. As a patterned form or schematism, it lies 'dead' before us, so to speak; it does not call out a response from us; "it does not point outside itself to a reality beyond... (Wittgenstein, 1981, no.236). So, how should we make sense of such meaningful activity? (p. 2)

Wittgenstein stressed that following the rules of a language is a certain kind of *doing*. It is not an act of thinking or really interpretation of a standard. It is matter of using publicly learned speaking in contexts where that speaking will receive a publicly trained response.

The point is we do not routinely respond in terms of already existing frameworks or rules external to our circumstances. We, on the other hand, respond spontaneously, without thought, to our contexts. We have learned this game. We speak and respond in characteristic ways. We practice doing it as an athlete might practice running. We live within "mingling streams" of activity. The patterns of these mingling streams form what might be called life's "logical grammar."

This would be a logical grammar of our forms of life. Shotter said:

> ...it is the seemingly arbitrary, ungrounded, and in fact not very systematic grammars structuring the background streams of activity (forms of life) within which we are inextricably involved, which provide the grounds for everything sensible we do and say (p. 2).

What is important about such a view is that what is understood and clear to members inside the context in which the activity is taking place is not necessarily understood or clear to those outside the context. Participation in the context is required. The context is critical.

Further this is quite a different approach than having an outsider look for something like "central constructs of meaning" or "internalized speech patterns." It (the above approach) does not look for anything hidden at all. As Wittgenstein pointed out: "...nothing is hidden...all is in plain view (PI 435)." What actually must be discovered and learned is "how to do it."

This is not the routine approach of science. There, a common practice is to develop theories, models, or schema of interpretation. For example, one is energized by one's Id. One responds to interpersonal cuing profiles, one internalizes object relations or "learned response patterns." These theoretical constructs are "hidden" in the sense we cannot readily observe them. Instead, we offer hypotheses and analyses about them. We then set about to amass evidence concerning our hypotheses and theories.

At other times we seek to amass evidence to support the personality elements, structures, and "pathologies" that warrant a diagnosis of, say, obsessive-compulsive personality disorder or ADHD. We want to know if a person "has" such a disorder.

We argue about all these matters. Who has the most evidence? The best evidence?

Even in social construction-ism, discursive psychology, conversational analysis, enthnomethodology, and other kindred enterprises, we have no hesitation in talking of unitary hypothetical entities – such as narratives, frameworks, rule structures, relational scenarios, language-games, etc. – which (once constructed) either function as special arenas or sites within which certain processes take place, or are assumed to exist as entities (things) which exert a determining force of some kind on people's behavior. (Shotter, P 3)

Further, we proceed in this fashion as if there were no other option. Of course, we think, we have to have a theoretical construct upon which to ground our structure, our interpretation.

A problem with this approach is that we must learn vast networks of unobservable constructs and theoretical interpretations in order to "under-

stand" people in light of those theories and interpretations. Everything that matters is, as it were,
hidden from view. These things must be interpreted into view or described into view in order for
them to be, as it were, *present*.

According to Wittgenstein's view, however, we
don't need theoretical constructs or interpretation
schema in order to learn and comprehend the alive
forces that pass between us and how we deal with
these forces. We have trouble not responding to
someone's anguish, someone's arrogance, or
someone's great joy. We don't hunt for interpretation schema to use in interpreting these things before we know what they are or how to respond.

Indeed, if this view is correct, and everything is
in plain view--and that people display their supposed mental states in their responses and reactions to what is going on about them, then "there
is nothing to theorize about, nothing to explain."
The task becomes, rather, to grasp the "grammar"
of the situation and to learn about the influence of
the context in which it is occurring.

Furthermore, such grammar is not responsible to
any reality beyond its own. That is, being the way

things are done in this context, grammar rests on no hidden property or theoretical metaphysic, sacred or not.

I know this is red, because I speak English.

I know Alice is hiding something, because I have begun to learn the grammar of her stilted presentation (her ways).

Different from the theoretical approaches descending from Descartes, understanding what we "mean," "understand," or "have in mind" does not require special techniques to search for hidden mental processes involved. We must, rather, understand the grammar of our interactions with our contexts.

Wittgenstein said:

> ...what we lack, he says, is "a clear view of our use of words," and "a perspicuous representation" produces just that under-standing which consists in 'seeing connections'" (PI, 122).

The understanding sought here is not laid out in systematic fashion on the page. It is demonstrated in our practical activities, in our ability to "do it too."

This approach represents a stage in the developmental progress from the static, mechanical world that could be observed from without to the dynamic two-way interactive world in which the observer is a co-creator.

Further there is a difference between studying something that is not alive from studying something that is alive.

Living beings are in a constant state of development. Consequently, to understand living things requires a consideration of their history, changes in context, and range of experience. This historical information interacts with present interpersonal and context related factors. In other words, we come with our histories, and our histories interact with our presents. (We come with strings attached.)

The Ubersichtlichte Darstellung ("perspicuous representation") allows us to "see the connections." This is the process we use when getting to know a new language or getting to know a new person. It is most certainly *not* to learn about a jumble of disjointed parts but a way to see how elements combine and influence each other. It is, in short, to learn their *grammar*.

There has long been a tension between "objective" science and what might be called "ordinary life." This distinction is, as it were, a hand-me-down of the era in which the mind and conceptual issues were prioritized and valorized over the body--which was largely deemed to be a fallible impediment to purity.

It is easy to see why this notion of scientific "objectivity" is not so. The "objectivity" supposed is, as Foucault (1970) indicated, heavily influenced by the context in which the "objectivity" takes place. That is the same elephant appears differently to ants, depending upon their location, era, sensibility level, &c.

In fact, among the many ways of going about accounting for something, it may be seen that empirical science is simply one of those ways. A "way of living" if you will. Further the procedure of taking objects of study out of their naturally occurring environments in order to see them more clearly adds a profound contamination of its own. This contamination is similar to subjecting ordinary occurring behaviors that have their own grammar (e.g., "smiles") out of their natural contexts and "defining" them (e.g., using "operational definitions" that may specify, for example, "the rising of the corners of the mouth five centimeters") . But, clearly, five centimeters doth not a smile make.

Such distorting procedures are questionably suited to an understanding of what it is to be *human*.

To be human is to be a natural person with a natural language in a naturally occurring context. No "definitions" or technical constructs are required.

A further point related to understanding naturally occurring phenomena is the notion of "sensibility."

When one first visits a city, one explores it--even if one has a map.   One goes down this street, crosses over to that one, visits a famous church. One is "getting to know" the city.   After two or three trips to the city, one's comprehension of the city has improved.   One may still get lost, but one "knows" the city better.   One's familiarity is greater.   One sees more.   One's sensibility has improved.

One might visit many cities, allowing for comparisons between them and the city first visited. Again one's sensibility has improved.   One may study the history of the city--the history of cities-- and one's sensibility further improves.

Like this, one may not know which of three paintings on a wall is a masterpiece.   One might wonder how others can tell?   In this case one hasn't developed the sensibility to see.

Elements of such a sensibility include a developed discrimination, sensitivity, knowledge base, and wide experience.   One has, as it were, to learn the city.   One needs to "know" it.

It is easy to see that such development does not require "operational definitions," central hidden constructs, or "conceptual maps."

It is also easy to see a similar procedure is employed when learning about another person, as is done in psychotherapy.

None of this is to suggest objective methods don't have a place. The explosion of knowledge due to such methods is vital. Like quantum theory, such methods may not fit well with anything else, but quantum theory makes possible a range of things that would not be possible without it (e.g., electronics).

In fact theoretical constructs, hidden or not, can all be adequately described in the ordinary language anyway. If this were not the case, they--like propositional calculus--could not be learned in the first place.

The problem with theoretical constructs is that they tend to become seen as "real." They may become seen as more real than the human qualities that lie behind them--qualities they were invented

to account for. Then we may be treating a "pathological category" instead of a human being.

IV

   The notion we are participants in a form of life
who speak a language that is meaningful in terms
of the grammar of our contexts suggests we are
participants who know how to do things. This is
what makes us human. Yet, while we all have an
experience of being human, we don't have the
same sorts of experiences within that humanity.

   Some of us are religious; some are not. Some of
us live in constant pain; some don't. Some are
Italian, American, rich, poor, factory workers,
dope addicts. we are old, young, &c.

   Though it may be said these are all human
things, they may be said to be different sorts of
human things. They are different ways to live or
"ways of living." It is different to live as a devout
religious person than to live as a devious busi-

nessman. In this fashion, ways of living provide for different contexts within the greater context of forms of life.

One might spend all of one's life in one town. This would allow for a fairly intimate understanding and attachment to develop to people and places over time that could certainly be meaningful, and deeply so, in its own right.

One might, on the other hand, spend one's life visiting as many towns as one can all over the world. This would allow for a different sort of view, one, say, in which differences blend and contrast.

These are two possible "ways of living" within the human "form of life."

People who pursue different ways of living are typically able to understand each other in any but a most superficial way only after a period of learning. This is, for example, how we can learn another language. The new language will not be a native language. We will learn the new language by learning different ways to say things we already know how to say in our native language.

But to be very proficient, we will also have to learn a good deal about the context in which the new language rose and flourishes.

The analogy holds for learning about another person. When we learn about another person we must learn about the contexts involved in their ways of living and how the person went about learning how to do the things they did and do within such contexts. We might ask, "What did it mean to do that where you came from (i.e., what "significance" did it have)?" We ask ourselves how does their experience differ from our own? Their parents were warm. My parents were un-available, &c.

One learns a language by practicing it. Similarly one learns how to live in one's context by practic-ing it. One learns *how to do it*. When this original context comes into collision with other contexts-- as all do more or less--new learning is required. One's way of living is different from another's way of living. There are similarities and differ-ences. One's original context has left one equipped to be more or less flexible, more or less curious, more or less defensive or closed off. One is optimistic; one is pessimistic.

434

Early contexts provide a wide range of physical experiences, emotional experiences, as well as varying degrees of focus on language learning and use.

Since it does not make sense there could (logically) be the *right way* of living (unless that is it is proclaimed by self definition or autocratic power), each way of living (like ways in which a pyramid can be seen) has similar logical status. Since this is the case, an obvious move would be to experience many different ways of living in order to improve one's sensibility about life.

That is, all ways of living are possibilities in the human form of life. A rich quilt.

For this reason, there is always 1) what you know, and 2) what lies beyond what you know.

Some people are eager to experience more of what they don't know. That is to involve themselves in and experience many different ways of living. Others find this frightening and seek to block out all knowledge of other ways of living, preferring to valorize their own. And so on.

It is not uncommon to encounter people who are "stuck" in a way of living. These people refuse to consider other forms. Often such ways are ridiculed or become victims of alterity. Eliad (1957, 1956; Little, 1942/1967) among others have suggested human culture evolved out of this kind of situation. Ancient person bonded with his tribe and sought to protect it from all others. Such a procedure was necessary for survival.

The logic was: my tribe versus yours. What was unknown was feared.

It can be seen that a similar sort of organization can be required for survival on a personal level, especially in an alien or hostile context.

> If we come to believe that what others require from us is at odds from who we 'really' are then we are likely to perform for them in a way which we know to be a lie as far as our 'real' self is concerned, and we can withdraw so far from this performance as to delight in our

capacity to act as an automaton and to fool others into believing that this is really us…However, what happens to our internal world is…more disastrous…removed from the requirement to check our ideas and feelings against the perceptions of others, we can all-to-easily become delusional, whether in terms of fantasies of omnipotence, or in terms of more subtle fantasies which provide us with a self-image which may deviate by a small or great amount from our actual qualities (Corker, p. 4).

We are entering an era in the history of culture when this procedure of protecting ourselves from all others at any cost is increasingly problematical. We are entering, in short, an era in which it is increasingly important for us to interact and get along with each other.

People who refuse to consider ways of living beyond their own may be said to be living in a "bubble," like a "bubble baby." The goal of such people appears to be shutting out other options in order to restrict focus to their own. The LDS people, for example, are fond of saying: "I don't need to learn anything else, because I already have the truth."

The obvious problem with living in a bubble is that one deprives oneself of an external view. That is, one may know (to some degree) where one is, but one is unable to experience where one is not. The result of this situation is that one does not know where one stands in the whole. In-bubble perceptions and experiences--being unchecked by outside input may drift in restricted and biased ways.

Bubble people appear in psychotherapy. There it may be discovered how they learned and practiced becoming bubble people.

Thinking about forms of life, ways of living, and bubbles helps one realize that there is an inherent limitation to what any one person can possible know or experience. The positive side of such a realization is one is able to position oneself with others in the form of life.

438

In this way forms of life are similar to forms of food or forms of painting. No single seasoning, no single template will successfully address them all.

And similarly in psychotherapy, one's theory, one's favorite area of study, one's lens, likely distorts as much as it clarifies.

V.

Growth requires an expansion from one's original context or way of life. Further, it is an axiom of post-modernism that things look different from different perspectives. It is routine that the problems we face in our life occur, in part, because we cannot see ways beyond them or options to them. Frequently the experience or realization we need to have in order to solve the problem we have is simply not available in our present context.

The more experiences we have in different perspectives, the more able we are to utilize those different experiences in dealing with our lives. This is to expand one's sensibility. We are enormously aided in this enterprise by working with a therapist who, by definition, comes from a different context. A therapist trained in an awareness of how difficult it is to shift perspectives can provide support and provide encouragement as we discover what is necessary to allow for such an expansion.

As people become more practiced and adept at shifting perspectives or ways of living, such developments become easier. Still, the most difficult task is to help someone move out of a bubble. Bubbles routinely contain both conscious and unconscious prohibitions against any serious movement away from them.

Persons trapped in bubbles are severely limited in the experiences of life available to them. Such a situation makes meaningful and rewarding interactions with others outside the bubble difficult if not impossible. Alterity is routine.

For this reason, there can be no accurate perspective. The goal of learning is not (necessarily) to increase accuracy or support for a particular perspective. The goal of learning is to increase the number of perspectives available to one.

Even so, one will be limited by one's time and the kinds of perspectives afforded in it. One's opportunities to experience can only extend so far.

It is another person who can help us learn about a view beyond our own--but it must be another person from a different context. If not the view of the other will likely be from an incestuous town where there is only one magazine for sale and only one tune on the juke-box.

Said Ogden (1989):

> As analysts, we attempt to assist the analysand [patient] in his efforts at freeing himself from forms of organized experience (his conscious and unconscious "knowledge" of himself) that entrap him and prevent him from tolerating the experience of not knowing long enough to create understandings in a different way. The value of developing new ways of

knowing lies not simply in the greater self-understanding one might achieve, but as importantly in the possibility that a wider range of thoughts, feelings, and sensations might be brought into being (p. 1)

A person who has been taught to "never leave home" or to "never leave one's family," will be required to develop defenses to gate out input from "the world beyond," that is from beyond home. If one's goal is to remain loyal to home at any cost, one has forfeited one's opportunity to grow in any synoptic way.

Of course, any therapist--being human (hopefully)--will have limitations as well.

These points may be illustrated by reference to a patient who, though a licensed professional, is painfully shy and suffers from significant fear of negative reactions from others—negative reactions, furthermore which he imagines to be everywhere.

The patient, Dr. P, described a demanding and overpowering mother who was deathly afraid of "society." She had enwrapped Dr. P. as a child in her fear and routinely cautioned him about the dangerous world outside. She set herself up as an authority against those who would disagree with her. We might say she "stunted" her child. The father was absent. When I met him Dr P was in his fifties, and his mother still terrified him. He dared not incur her wrath.

Dr. P had come out of a context in which he felt inadequate and chronically fearful of attack. Yet there was another element. He was (unconsciously) taught it was unthinkable to leave home--or abandon his mother's influence. His mother convinced him she was right and to oppose her was wrong. This was his foundation, from which he was attempting to conduct an adult life.

If you will, this is the grammar of his way of life, his "life game."

Furthermore, Dr. P had spent a good deal of time with several therapists before I met him. They all noticed his intransigence, his stubbornness even in the face of a clear desire to improve, and his irrationality on this point.

There are clearly many ways to think about Dr. P. His self-view is severely negatively focused and results in him projecting his mother onto other persons. (He thus projects a "critical audience.") His core beliefs are not rational or helpful.

An approach would be to join him in his childhood perception and help him learn what was not present there. This would include a view of his mother as frightened and overwhelmed as well as a realization that no one else in his life saw him the way his mother did. He, however, had no option as a child. The therapeutic context could provide such an option—without the dreaded negative reactions. It could even include warmth and genuine regard.

The patient could be helped to learn the difference between the therapeutic situation and his imagined "world." This would be to help Dr. P. have an *experience* of a different *way of living*.

Within this different experience Dr. P. could experience himself being treated and thought of differently. He could begin to learn his mother was not big and powerful as he had perceived her, but frightened and inadequate. Again, within this different empathic and supportive context, Dr. P. could begin to experience other people as NOT being as his mother. This would allow for more positive and rewarding interactions between himself and other people.

In other words, if a therapist were able to learn enough about Mr. P's context to "join" him tolerably so an immediate sort of empathy could be established, the therapist could rely as well on his or her own different, and hopefully more analyzed, development to help the patient. Together they could move through the patient's development to date and discover options that could have taken place if there were not such a mother.

Refusing to, or claiming an inability to, move beyond mother's sphere could be thought of as the survival stance of a child who is overwhelmed, frightened, and lacking support. "Transgressions" in this area could be contained and metabolized. Finally, the patient could be encouraged (and supported) for encouraging yet further contexts beyond the world of his mother and the world as well of his past experience.

A recent article by Judith Beck takes a different tack. The title of this article was "Using Socratic Questioning to help social anxiety."

> My client, I'll call her Alison, has social anxiety. Like many people with her problem, she holds a strong belief: "I shouldn't call attention to myself." Alison believes at heart that there is something inherently wrong with her, something that could potentially lead people to find her unappealing. Therefore, she believes she should control her behavior and not do anything that could result in criticisms from other people. I asked Alison if she was willing to do a behavioral experiment to see what would happen, for example, if she asked a question in the large office or staff meeting or made conversation with a stranger

in a crowded elevator. She was a
bit horrified at these suggestions.

Is "holding a belief" ("holding an apple") the
same thing as "believing strongly?"

At any rate to deal with this erroneous belief, the
therapist recalled to the patient a personal experience of her own. This involved an assertive act
and the possibility onlookers would have negative
reactions to it or to her.

"That was really brave," Alison said.
"Thanks," I replied, "but I didn't
think so. I might have when I was
much younger, and shyer--but I
would have been wrong. It truly
wasn't a big deal." I paused, to give
her time to reflect on what I said.
"What do you think?"

The two then discussed possible criticisms people could have had of Judith. "Would they have
been right?" was the question asked.

Having established "they" were not "right," or not "necessarily" "right," the therapist asked:

> If someone has a critical opinion, does that necessarily reflect badly on me? Could it say more about the personality of the person doing the criticizing?

Here the therapist attempts to get the patient to see the situation from a different perspective. The therapist also tries to get the patient to imagine a situation that would be daunting to the patient.

> ...let's say you're in a crowded elevator and you start making conversation about the weather with someone," I said. "One person thinks, "That's nice that she's--that is, you--are reaching out to say something." A second person thinks, "Why is she saying that? I

don't want to talk to her."   Who is
right?

Alison here responded that it is possible the
terms "right" and "wrong" might not apply, and
the therapist takes the "questioning" one step farther.

"If you do the experiment of starting
conversations in the elevator, do you
change from an okay person before
you get in the elevator to a not okay
person if the second woman criti-
cizes you"

"No, I guess not."

Now Alison is considering the situation differently, the point of the encounter was summed up
as follows:

This discussion, a typical example of
the Socratic questioning process in

cognitive therapy, guides the client to evaluate her assumptions and modify her thinking so she can reach her goals. In the following weeks, Alison not only spoke up in elevators and staff meetings but also initiated conversations in public places such as bookstores and at social gatherings. She received mostly positive or neutral reactions from people, which helped erode the idea that there was something wrong with her.

Magic.

A more involved analysis of the above incident would yield (among other things) the following points. If Alison has "social anxiety," she has a far more involved and significant problem than "a strong belief." What has been her way of living? How did she learn to have this pattern? How did she practice? What about the context of her childhood home? Who else in her family had social anxiety? Why? How did society get to be scary? How was it Alison learned to rely on the opinions of others instead of her own judgment?

What is the "grammar" of her anxiety?

Where did she get the thought there is something wrong with her, something other people would find unappealing? How did her esteem become damaged? How was this taught? Where are her friends? Who loves her?

And when Alison came to see the therapist, she certainly came to see someone quite different from the people in her background. How is the therapist different? For one thing, Alison is a scared and unsure person. The therapist is confident and capable. She might have diplomas all over her walls. Her office may be in an important building. There is a formality involved. The therapist is a "doctor."

What is being described in the above example is a situation in which the patient is helped to see from a different perspective--which is *not* a "cognitive process" but another sort of *experience*.

It is certainly arguable that the outcome is attributable to the nature of the new therapeutic experiences Alison has had and how they impact her current way of living. In the above example Alison is actually interacting with a person from a different way of living from her own. That is, the therapist has had different experiences and thus it is reasonable to assume she also has different assumptions and expectations--not simply a different *belief.*

If Alison has been living for a long time with her "social anxiety," it is likely she has been caught in a bubble. And while it may be the case she was able to be more openly social following this above described encounter with a therapist, there are many aspects of her situation that have not been considered here.

What, for example, is Alison going to do with her way of living now? What is she going to do with her relationships? What about the niche she occupies at work? What about the Alison her colleagues conjure? What will be possible with them? What about her long standing worries about her own worth? What of her view of herself? What of her view of others? What about her perception of her place in the world? What of her dreams?

If the therapist thinks Alison is improved--because perhaps that fits the therapist's bubble--is she actually improved? What would improved be? Would it be meaningful, deeply-rewarding, and lasting relationships? Would it be the ability to come out of the cake at the party?

What would we encounter were *we* to get to know Alison? How would we find her at six months? A year? What is Alison's great wish? What does her wounded self have to tell us? At what point might we say we understand Alison very well?

A therapist's job is to learn how another person "does life." How does he or she practice what he or she is doing? And since none of us can come to any sort of expanded awareness by ourselves (we must work with another) it is important that we not come from a restrictive way of living only to encounter another restrictive way of living in the therapist.

This is why the therapist cannot be "the expert." "Expert" at what? Applying theories? Reciting (empirically collected) evidence?

Nancy McWilliams (1994) stressed the "path to the self lies through the other." The self we imagine now first lay through our parents and what they saw and imagined about us. The therapist's view is *different*. It is not *right*. (Whatever that might be.)

Clearly, contexts promulgate some interpretations, some ways of seeing, over others. What is valued in one place is denounced in another.

Our lives are made healthier when we have the opportunity to *discover*, without undue bias or limitation how we can best flourish. As therapists we are most helpful when we aid others in doing just this. The preparation for becoming such a therapist is, in addition to one's own therapy, to also become cosmopolitan in knowledge and experience so what is naturally occurring is not distorted by formal constructs or unfortunate narrowness and bias of outlook.

And that is the story of forms, ways, perspectives, and bubbles.

REFERENCES

Anderson, H.   Conversation, Language, and Possibilities. Basic, 1997.

Angelo, R.W.   http://www.roangelo.net/logwitt/
logwitt5.html 2008.

Beck, J.S.   Using Socratic Questioning to Help
Social Anxiety. The Huffington Post. 10-11-10.

Biletzki, A. and Matar, A. "Ludwig Wittgenstein,"
The Stanford Encyclopedia of Philosophy.   Summer, 2011, Section 2.1.

Blair, D.C. Wittgenstein, language and information: 'back to the rough ground!' Springer. 2006

Bower, B.   Darwin's Tongues.   In Science News.
11-19-2011. pp. 21-25.

Curry, M.R.   Wittgenstein and the Fabric of Everyday Life. In M. Crang and N. Thrift (Eds.) In Thinking Space. Routledge. 2000.

Derrida, J.   Of Grammatology. Johns Hopkins. 1976.

Eliade, M. The Sacred and the Profane: The Nature of Religion. Harcourt. 1957.

Eliade, M. Myth and Reality. Harper. 1963,

Eliot, T.S.   Sweeney Agonistes (Sweeney Agonistes: Fragments of an Aristophanic Melodrama). Faber and Faber. 1932.

Flax. J. Thinking Fragments: Psychoanalysis, Feminism, and Postmodernism in the Contemporary West. California. 1990.

Fausto-Sterling, A. Sexing the Body: Gender Politics and the Construction of Sexuality.   Basic. 2000.

Foucault, M. The Order of Things: An Archaeology of the Human Sciences.   Random House. 1970.

Foucault, M. The History of Sex (Vol I). Random House. 1978.

Gadamer, H,G. *Truth and Method*, 2nd rev. edn., trans. by J. Weinsheimer and D.G.Marshall, Crossroad, 1989.

Heiddegger, M. Existence and Being. Gateway. 1949.

Little, A.M.G. Myth and Society in Attic Drama. Octagon. 1942/1967.

Lyotard, J.-F., *The Postmodern Condition: A Report on Knowledge*, G. Bennington and B. Massumi (trans.), Minnesota, 1984.

Malcom, N. Ludwig Wittgenstein: A Memoir. Oxford. 1958.

Ogden, T.H. The Primitive Edge of Experience. Aronson. 1989.

Pitcher, G. The Philosophy of Wittgenstein. Prentice-Hall. 1964.

Shotter, J. Wittgenstein and the Everyday: From Radical Hiddenness to Nothing is Hidden; from Representation to Participation. http://pub-pages.unh.edu/~jds/JMB.htm

Web http://en.wikipedia.org/wiki/Form_of_life_(philosophy Eliot sweeny)

Witt-1 http://plato.stanford.edu/entries/wittgen-stein/

Witt-2 http://www.sparknotes.com/philosophy/wittgenstein/section3.rhtml

Witt-3 (http://www.sparknotes.com/philosophy/wittgenstein/section3.rhtml)

Wittgenstein, L. Philosophical Investigations, (Trans G.E.M. Anscombe). Macmillan. 1953.

Wittgenstein,L. Zettel. (Ed.) G.E.M. Anscombe. Blackwell, 1967.

Wittgenstein, L. Tractatus Logico-Philosophicus. (Trans.) D.F Pears and B.F. MacGuinness. Rout-ledge. 1974,

Wittgenstein, L. Culture and Value, (Trans.) P. Winch. Oxford: Blackwell. 19

ABOUT THE AUTHOR

J.D. Gill is a clinical psychologist at the University of Utah. She is an Adjunct Associate Professor of Psychology, a Clinical Professor of Counseling Psychology, and an Adjunct Associate Professor of Psychiatry in the University of Utah School of Medicine. Dr. Gill maintains a busy practice at the University of Utah Neuropsychiatric Institute.

Dr. Gill has degrees in English Literature, Philosophy, and two post docs in psychoanalytic psychotherapy. She studied in the Writing Program at the University of Utah. She has been a practicing psychologist for over forty years and has presented over five hundred seminars, lectures, workshops, and papers. A world traveler, Dr. Gill has actively sought to experience multiple viewpoints and perspectives.

www.ingramcontent.com/pod-product-compliance
Lightning Source LLC
Chambersburg PA
CBHW070408290526
45791CB00005B/1678